ROY BENNETT
formerly Head of Music and Drama at
Buckler's Mead School, Yeovil

Enjoying music

BOOK 3

LONGMAN

How an orchestra is laid out

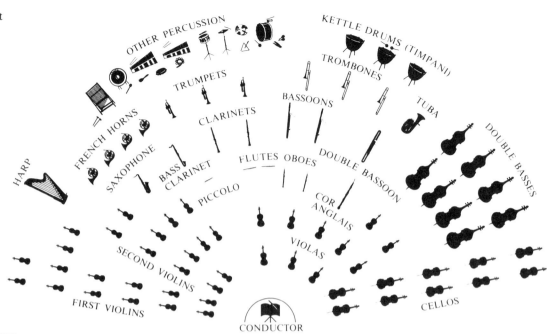

The Hallé Orchestra under
its conductor, James Loughran

Emmanuel Chabrier FRANCE 1841-1894

Rhapsody: España

Although Chabrier always wanted to become a musician, his father decided that music was too uncertain a career for him. He became a civil servant instead and was nearly forty before he decided to give up his post and devote all his time to music.

Chabrier had a flair for writing attractive tunes, then orchestrating them in fresh, glowing colours. His music was so easy to listen to that audiences would not take him seriously, so sometimes he tried to compose music of a more serious nature. But it is still his lighter pieces – the *Marche Joyeuse* (the title fits the music perfectly!) and the *Rhapsody: España* ('Spain') – which are most often played. Before Chabrier wrote *España*, he visited Spain and jotted down folk tunes which attracted him. A friend said later: 'Chabrier soon made friends with the dancers. He drank *manzanilla* with them, clapped his hands as the Andalusians twisted their hips, and cried out: "Olé! Olé" '.

Points to listen for

1. An introduction on *pizzicato* strings and woodwind, with triangle and tambourine, gradually builds up – then launches into:
2. The first tune (**A**) on muted trumpet. This is a *jota* – a fast Spanish dance. It is repeated: first *pp*; then, suddenly, *ff*.
3. Tune **B** is played with a terrific swing by four French horns.
4. Trumpets and trombones cut through with brilliant explosions from the percussion, followed by a light-hearted dance for bassoon.
5. Tune **C** is shared between violins and clarinets. This is a *malagueña* – a dance from the province of Malaga, famous for its delicious grapes and wines. Tune **C** is repeated by the woodwind.
6. Strings take the next tune (**D**) above a rumble of kettledrums.
7. Against a shimmering harp background, trombones blare out Tune **E**. Woodwind instruments reply by dancing the *jota* (Tune **A**).
8. After an outburst – with a good deal of noise from brass and kettledrums – we hear all these tunes again, except the bassoon tune.
9. Eventually, the tambourine taps out the *jota* rhythm while the brass plays Tune **E**. Then the music builds up to an exciting climax – a vivid picture of colour and movement.

A drawing of Chabrier at the piano

Dancing the *jota*

French horn

muted trumpet

trombone

tambourine

3

Paul Dukas FRANCE 1865-1935

The Sorcerer's Apprentice

Dukas is an example of what we might call a 'one-work composer', for although he wrote a great deal of music, *The Sorcerer's Apprentice* is his only piece which is often played at concerts nowadays. Even so, when he conducted its first performance in Paris in 1897, he became famous almost overnight.

All Dukas's known compositions were written before 1910. During that year he decided to give up writing music, and burned all those pieces he had written which were still unpublished. But in 1913 he became Professor of Composition at the famous college of music in Paris called the *Conservatoire*, and taught several important French musicians there until his death in 1935.

Orchestras really enjoy playing *The Sorcerer's Apprentice*, as during this piece every instrument has something interesting and challenging to play. Dukas calls his piece a 'Scherzo for Orchestra'. (*Scherzo* is Italian for 'a joke'.)

The story

Dukas wrote *The Sorcerer's Apprentice* after reading a poem by the German writer, Goethe. It tells the story of a rather lazy apprentice who is told to fill a huge cauldron with water while his master, the Sorcerer, goes out on important business. The day is hot; the Apprentice sleepy. Suddenly he has an idea. He will cast a spell upon the broom so that it will fetch the water – while he has a rest.

The spell is cast. The broom begins to twitch into life. It grows arms and legs, snatches up a pair of buckets, and disappears. Seconds later it returns, and begins to fill the cauldron. Well pleased with himself, the Apprentice falls into a doze . . .

Suddenly, he wakes up. Water is lapping around his ankles. The cauldron is overflowing! He must stop the spell – but he cannot remember the magic words! Desperately, he seizes an axe and splits the broom in two. But each half grows into a whole new broom! Each of them snatches up buckets, and disappears. Then, to the Apprentice's horror, the two brooms become four. The four become eight. Soon a whole army of brooms is bringing water into the castle!

The Apprentice is swimming for dear life when, to his relief, the Sorcerer returns. Powerful magic words are pronounced – and all returns to normal. Only the question of punishment remains . . .

The French composer, Paul Dukas

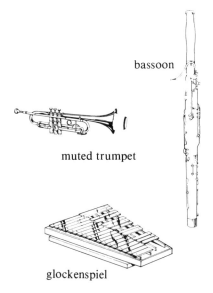

muted trumpet

glockenspiel

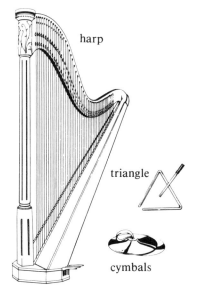

bassoon

harp

triangle

cymbals

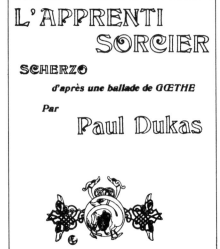

L'APPRENTI SORCIER

SCHERZO

d'après une ballade de GŒTHE

Par

Paul Dukas

Points to listen for

1. Violins and flutes picture the dreamy Apprentice (Tune **A**). In bar 3, the clarinet, then other woodwind instruments, play the theme of the broom – at present standing quietly in the corner. This is repeated.

2. The music quickens, as the idea dawns in the Apprentice's mind.

3. The magic spell theme (**B**) on muted trumpets and French horns.

4. Silence! Then the broom begins to twitch into life . . . The broom's theme is played on three bassoons (**C**).

5. A great deal is heard of Tunes **A** and **C** as the broom goes eagerly about its business.

6. Another tune (**D**) is heard on high woodwind and glockenspiel. (The clear, silvery sounds of glockenspiel, harp and triangle are often heard in this piece of music.)

7. The music becomes more excited as the cauldron overflows. Water splashes everywhere and rushing scales suggest the rising level – waking up the Apprentice who tries in vain to stop the magic (Tunes **A** and **B** alternately).

8. Crashing chords as he chops the broom in half! But double bassoon, then bass clarinet, indicate that both halves are beginning to move. Theme **C** again on the bassoons; then higher, on clarinets.

9. The music gradually rises to even greater fury. Later, bass drum and cymbals, as the brooms begin to multiply and water splashes everywhere. Then Tune **A** as water cascades through the entire castle!

10. The Sorcerer returns! Tune **B** – overwhelmingly powerful – as he pronounces the magic words necessary to break the spell. Instantly, the water vanishes.

11. Tunes **A** and **C** sadly reflect the unfortunate Apprentice . . . .

12. And the final brisk chords firmly suggest a sharp box on the ears!

flute   piccolo

Dukas uses quite a large orchestra for this music: 2 flutes and piccolo, 2 oboes, 2 clarinets and bass clarinet, 3 bassoons and double bassoon; 4 horns, 2 trumpets, 2 cornets, and 3 trombones; 3 kettledrums, bass drum, cymbals, triangle, glockenspiel; harp; and strings.

The Sorcerer's Apprentice, with Mickey Mouse in the title-role, was one of the pieces featured in Walt Disney's film, *Fantasia*

Richard Strauss GERMANY 1864-1949

Till Eulenspiegel

Richard Strauss was the first composer to become a millionaire from royalties earned by writing music. Whereas some composers may have starved while writing their greatest music, Strauss was very highly paid for his compositions. A symphony he wrote in 1902 immediately brought him £1750, while a quickly written song could easily fetch £50 – and this at a time when a weekly wage of 25 shillings (£1.25) was considered a good one.

Strauss's childhood contrasts sharply with that of many other composers. His father was first horn-player in the Munich Court Opera Orchestra; his mother was heiress to a brewery fortune. So there were both money and music in his background – and more than enough of each. And not only was he encouraged, but he was also expected, to make a career in music. At first he studied under private teachers, all carefully selected by his musical father. By the age of seventeen he had already written several promising pieces of music, including a *Serenade for Wind Instruments* which is still sometimes performed today.

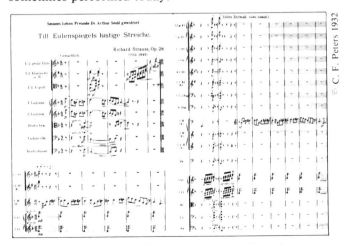

Till Eulenspiegel: the opening pages of the orchestral score

Richard Strauss at the age when he composed *Till Eulenspiegel*

When the famous conductor, Hans von Bülow, heard the young Strauss conduct his *Serenade* he was so impressed that he offered him the post of deputy conductor. From then on Strauss followed the twin careers of composer and conductor, gaining equal success in both. For many years he was Director of the Berlin State Opera, and later of the Vienna State Opera. Strauss was still conducting at public concerts when he was well into his eighties.

Although he wrote several operas, and a great many *Lieder* (songs), Strauss is best known for his *symphonic poems*. (A *symphonic poem* is an orchestral piece which tells a story or paints a picture in sound.) These pieces include *Don Juan* (the legendary great lover), *Till Eulenspiegel, Also sprach Zarathustra* (partly used as music for the film *2001 Space Odyssey*, and also as signature tune for television programmes of the Apollo moonshots), *Don Quixote* (based on a story about a crazy knight, by the Spanish writer Cervantes), and *Ein Heldenleben*, or 'A Hero's Life' – the hero, of course, being Strauss himself!

An old print of Till on horseback, holding an owl and a looking-glass

French horn

clarinet

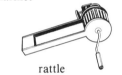

rattle

Strauss in his eighties, composing at the piano

The full title of Strauss's piece is *Till Eulenspiegels lustige Streiche* ('Till Eulenspiegel's Merry Pranks'). The music tells of the adventures of a medieval rogue who gained a wide reputation for playing practical jokes. Countless stories grew up about his tricks and exploits, which were usually directed against wealthy or pompous people to make them look ridiculous. As this usually afforded amusing entertainment for any onlookers, it is easy to understand why Till was really quite a popular character.

In German, *Eulenspiegel* is an 'owl-glass', and the verb *eulenspiegeln* was coined from Till's name to mean 'to make a fool of someone'. There is still an old German proverb which observes that 'a man can no more see his own failings than an owl can recognise its ugliness by peering into a looking-glass'. At first, Strauss refused to give a detailed 'programme' of his piece, but later he pencilled rough notes into the score.

The story

Till, on horseback, rides recklessly through the crowded market-place, infuriating stall-holders by spilling fruit and vegetables, breaking crockery. He gaily rides off and hides.

Wearing the 'borrowed' robes of a priest, he preaches to a crowd of people. The Devil himself looks on and smiles in approval. But the village cobbler recognises one of Till's shoes peeping out from beneath his robes. Realising they have been taken in, the villagers angrily chase him away.

Now masquerading as a courteous knight, he makes advances towards a pretty girl, but she rejects him. He slinks away in fury, swearing vengeance on all mankind.

But his sense of humour returns as he makes fun of learned scholars by putting forward outrageous views; then slips away, leaving them to argue furiously among themselves.

But this time Till has gone too far. He is pursued, and captured. The gallows are raised. He is accused – and sentenced to death.

Most legends are rooted in fact. Like Grieg's Peer Gynt and Rossini's William Tell, Strauss's character Till Eulenspiegel actually lived. The real Till died at Mölln – though it is said that he died of the plague rather than in the spectacular way Strauss describes in his music. In the churchyard there you can still see a gravestone cut with Till's emblem – an owl and a looking-glass.

"Once upon a time..."

Strauss describes his music as a 'Rondo for Orchestra'. In a *rondo*, the main theme keeps 'coming round'. In this piece, it is Theme **A** which we keep hearing – but often in a disguised form – like Till himself! – as in Tunes **C**, **D** and **G**.

Points to listen for

1. Prologue. The mood seems to suggest: 'Once upon a time . . .' The main theme (**A**) is played thoughtfully by the strings, soon followed by Till's own theme, his 'signature' (**B**), on first French horn. It is heard again, then passed to other instruments: oboes, clarinets, then bassoons and lower strings. A burst of high spirits from the full orchestra, and a scrap of Theme **A** is mischievously played by a clarinet (**C**) as if Till suddenly leaps out in glee from behind a wall.

2. A passage beginning with a light, skipping rhythm shows him eagerly searching for adventure. Later, woodwind instruments imitate his carefree whistling.

3. Eventually, a new version of Theme **A** is heard (**D**), and the music becomes more stealthy as Till spies the crowded market-place and a horse tethered nearby . . . Then, a deafening outburst, helped considerably by a rattle (of the football variety) in the percussion section, and wildly neighing brass, as he dashes through – sending everything (and everybody) crashing to the ground.

4. He laughingly surveys the chaos he has caused, and woodwind instruments suggest him making rude signs – from a safe distance!

5. Disguised now as a priest, he approaches the villagers and begins his mock sermon (Tune **E**, on violas, clarinets and bassoons). The Devil smiles his approval (muted brass). But Till is recognised, and rips off his disguise to a light descending run on a solo violin.

6. The music becomes more lilting as swooning strings tell us that Till has fallen in love (**F**). But he is rejected, and shows his fury in a more decisive version of the main theme, played by the brass (**G**).

7. He approaches a group of scholars (Tune **H**, on bassoons and clarinets) and soon sets them arguing fiercely – indicated in the music by jerky rhythms, pulling against each other in disagreement. The argument becomes violent (brass and kettle drums). Till makes off again.

8. Then follows a lengthy section of music to which Strauss gives no clue as far as the story is concerned. Perhaps he leaves us to imagine for ourselves the tricks that Till will get up to! Listen for Till's theme again on the French horn (**B**); and later, Tune **E**, now much stronger on horns and trombones. At the end of this section the music becomes louder and faster. Justice is catching up with him . . . Then, suddenly, he is caught!

9. Above an ominous roll on a kettledrum, lower brass and woodwind thunder out the Judge's accusation. Till's cheeky reply is heard on the high-pitched clarinet in D. A second accusation; another reply – perhaps now not quite so confident? After the third accusation, Till's reply sounds like a desperate cry for mercy. But Justice knows no pity! He is sentenced to death by hanging. The Devil – so far Till's ally – now mocks him (muted brass). The noose is tightened (**I**) and we hear his terrified final shriek on the clarinet in D. *Pizzicato* strings suggest his death-twitches . . .

10. Epilogue. Theme **A** is heard once more, sounding even more wistful than at first. Till's own theme, heard afterwards, is now no more than a shadow . . . Then the music ends in a burst of high spirits: Till Eulenspiegel is dead – but his spirit of fun lives on!

Richard Strauss is especially noted for his vivid *orchestration* – that is, the way in which he selects and combines the various orchestral instruments which are to play his music, blending and contrasting their tone-qualities to make a brilliant and colourful orchestral sound. *Till Eulenspiegels lustige Streiche* requires a large orchestra, consisting of: piccolo, 3 flutes, 3 oboes, cor anglais, small clarinet in D, 2 clarinets, bass clarinet, 3 bassoons, double bassoon; 4 horns, 4 extra horns if possible, 3 trumpets, 3 extra trumpets if possible, 3 trombones, bass tuba; kettledrums, snare drum, bass drum, cymbals, triangle, a 'watchman's rattle'; and a large section of strings.

Legend has it that at the scene of each 'crime', Till's 'signature' would be found chalked up in the form of a drawing of an owl and a looking-glass.

Sergei Prokofiev U.S.S.R. 1891-1953
Suite of music from the film
Lieutenant Kijé

Prokofiev received his first piano lessons from his mother, and was writing short pieces by the time he was five. At thirteen, he began to attend the Conservatory of Music at St. Petersburg (now Leningrad) and took lessons in composition from the Russian composer, Rimsky-Korsakov.

Prokofiev's first serious compositions were too 'modern' for audiences at that time. His *Second Piano Concerto* was described as sounding like 'cats fighting in an alley', and at its first performance most of the audience walked out! But many of the pieces he wrote later, especially his ballet *Romeo and Juliet* and his 'Musical Tale for Children': *Peter and the Wolf*, contain attractive tunes. One of Prokofiev's 'finger-prints' is that he will give a tune a sudden 'twist', sending it into a distant key – usually, however, allowing it to return home again quite safely. (Tune **F**, opposite, is an example of this.)

In 1918, Prokofiev left Russia and stayed for some time in Europe and America. But in 1933 he decided to return to Russia. The first music he wrote after this was for the film *Lieutenant Kijé*.

Prokofiev composing at the piano

Prokofiev was one of the greatest masters of modern orchestration and achieved effects stunning in their force and expressiveness.

The Russian composer Khatchaturian

Scene from a ballet version of *Lieutenant Kijé*

The strangest fact about the film *Lieutenant Kijé* is that the whole story revolves around a character who just doesn't exist! It comes about in this way:

One day, as the Czar is reading a military report, he comes upon the words *'Parootchiki je . . .'*, which in Russian means 'The Lieutenants, however . . .'. But a blot of ink, carelessly dropped upon the paper, causes him to read instead *'Parootchi Kijé'*, meaning 'Lieutenant Kijé'. Now the Czar *cannot* be wrong – and so no one dares to correct him!

Intrigued by this unusual name, the Czar begins to make enquiries about the 'officer'. And so his advisers find themselves in the ridiculous situation of having to invent a whole series of brave adventures for the quite imaginary 'Lieutenant Kijé' . . .

1. The Birth of Kijé

Kijé is 'born' – fully-grown, of course – to a fanfare on a distant cornet (**A**); then immediately reports on parade to the rhythm of a snare drum and a carefree tune on a piccolo (**B**). Other instruments join the parade. There is another tune (**C**) which represents Kijé himself. The music ends with Tune **B**, and the fanfare on the cornet, now muted.

2. Romance

In the film-score, this is a love-song sung by a baritone:

My grey dove is full of sorrow,
Moaning is she day and night,
For her dear companion left her,
Having vanished out of sight . . .

To my heart I say: don't flutter,
Don't be like a butterfly . . .
But my heart could answer nothing,
Beating fast in my poor breast.

Prokoviev wrote a later version, however, for orchestra only, sharing the melody (**D**) between various instruments, including double bass, cello and tenor saxophone. The middle section is in the style of a very Russian slow dance.

3. The Wedding of Kijé

The full orchestra describes the solemn ceremony (**E**). Then we join the festivities at the wedding breakfast with a melody for cornet (**F**) above an 'oom-pah' accompaniment. Kijé's own theme (**C**) appears, then Tunes **F** and **E** alternate for the rest of the piece.

4. Troika

Another song – this time a Russian tavern song, but with an accompaniment describing a dashing sleigh-ride across the Russian plain.

A woman's heart is like an inn:
All those who wish go in.
And they who roam about
Day and night go in and out.
Come here, I say; come here, I say;
And have no fear with me.

Be you bachelor or not,
Be you shy, or be you bold,
I call you all to come here.
So all those who are about
Keep going in and coming out,
Night and day they roam about.

In the orchestral version, cellos and saxophones play Tune **G** against the exciting sounds of sleigh bells, triangle and tambourine. Besides Kijé's own theme (**C**) there are rhythmic tunes for brass (**H** and **I**).

5. The Burial of Kijé

So the time comes when Kijé must 'die' – but with full military honours! His whole career is reviewed: Tune **A** on the distant cornet is followed by Tune **C** on low clarinets, then saxophone. We are reminded of his love-song (**D**), later joined by his wedding-dance (**F**) – both tunes now played at the same time! But Kijé's own theme (**C**) naturally plays the most important part in the proceedings. Then, to the ghostly fanfare on the distant muted cornet (**A**), our hero is finally laid to rest . . .

saxophone

cornet

tambourine

sleigh bells

triangle

11

George Gershwin AMERICA 1898-1937

RHAPSODY IN BLUE

In 1924, the famous American band-leader, Paul Whiteman, organised a concert which he described as 'An Experiment in American Music'. He asked George Gershwin if he would like to write a 'jazz-influenced concert piece' for the occasion. At first, Gershwin didn't take Whiteman too seriously – so he received quite a shock when he read in the *New York Tribune* of January 4th that the concert was to take place on February 12th, mentioning in particular that 'George Gershwin is at work on a jazz concerto'. Gershwin decided he had better get down to work! A train journey to Boston brought musical ideas into his mind:

'It was on the train, with its steely rhythms, its rattly-bang that is so often stimulating to a composer, that I suddenly heard – even saw on paper – the complete construction of the Rhapsody *from beginning to end . . . I heard it as a sort of musical kaleidoscope of America – of our vast melting pot, of our incomparable national pep, our blues, our metropolitan madness.'*

New York in the 1920s

Self-caricature of Gershwin

The rhythms should be made to snap, at times to crackle. The more sharply the music is played, the more effective it sounds.

Gershwin sent the piano score to Whiteman in an unfinished state. Whiteman then asked another American composer, Ferde Grofé, to orchestrate the accompaniment for jazz band. But even at the actual concert there were blank pages in the piano part which Gershwin said he would improvise on the spot. Whiteman experienced some tense moments as he conducted – especially during one very long gap which simply carried the scribbled direction: 'Wait for nod'!

Later, Grofé took his original Jazz Band accompaniment and re-wrote it for full Symphony Orchestra. It is this version of *Rhapsody in Blue* that is usually performed nowadays.

In writing *Rhapsody in Blue*, Gershwin's aim had been to write a 'jazz-influenced concert piece'. The special tone-qualities of the accompanying instruments account, of course, for a great deal of its jazz flavour. But Gershwin uses two other main ingredients:

Jazz ingredients in Gershwin's music
Syncopation – a 'swinging' of the rhythm, but in particular by placing an emphasis on weak beats rather than on strong.
Blue Notes – the flattening of certain notes of the scale, especially the 3rd and the 7th. Notes marked + in the music below are key examples of this. Very often, the flattened 'blue note' in the *melody* clashes strongly with the same note, but unaltered, in the *harmony* beneath – as, for example, at the chords marked *.

Points to listen for

1. A spine-tingling clarinet *glissando* ('sliding') leads into Tune **A**.
2. Another important idea (Tune **B**) is first heard on the brass.
3. Tune **A**, now played by a trumpet with a 'wow-wow' mute, encourages the piano to enter with Tune **C**. The full orchestra repeats Tune **A** with loud cymbal clashes. The piano now elaborates Tune **C**; then launches into a *cadenza* (where the orchestra remains silent while the soloist shows off his technique with some dazzling playing).
4. Tune **A** on the piano, while a bass clarinet bubbles away between phrases with Tune **C**. The piano continues to explore Tunes **A** and **C**.
5. Tune **A** is now eagerly taken over by the full orchestra, *fortissimo*.
6. Tune **D** is punched out by trumpets against bright splashing chords from the piano.
7. Short solos for clarinet (**B**); then Tune **B** *fortissimo* on the full orchestra – with strong rhythms on the snare-drum – while the piano accompanies with stamping chords. This section ends with solo 'breaks' in blues style: first for clarinet, then trumpet, and finally trombone (these last two fitted with 'wow-wow' mutes).
8. (*In performance, this section is sometimes omitted.*) A baritone saxophone plays Tune **E** (similar at first to Tune **D**) while wood block and suspended cymbal steadily mark each beat. All this is vigorously repeated with bright-stabbing high octaves from the piano.
9. Piano solo: Tune **B**, with 'blue notes' and decorations. Later, a trombone joins in, gently moaning long-held notes in the background. Listen for Tune **A**, *fortissimo*, on the piano in rich, full chords.
10. Tune **E** on the solo piano, at first with the melody in the right hand *below* chords in the left. The texture becomes thicker, rhythmically more intricate.
11. A rich, romantic melody is introduced by saxophones and cellos (**F**). After a wistful violin solo, Tune **F** is repeated *fortissimo* with snare drum rolls, while the piano plays chords based on the figure marked *x*.
12. Piano solo: first figure *x* from Tune **F**. Then Tune **F**, rich and flowing – rather in the style of the Russian composer, Rachmaninov.
13. A sudden change of pace and mood – sharp, quickly-repeated notes on the piano. Listen for Tune **C** in the tenor register of the keyboard. This section ends with a brilliant upward *glissando*.
14. The brass plays Tune **F** in a quicker tempo with a *crescendo* on each long note. The piano glitters brightly in the background.

15. After a *fortissimo* raucous discord, the music begins to build up like a mighty wave. At the crest – Tune **B**, *fortissimo*, on the piano against decisive, punched chords on the full orchestra.
16. Tune **A**, *fortissimo*, with explosive cymbal clashes. Then, finally, Tune **C** – majestically drawn out on the piano, and marked *fff*.

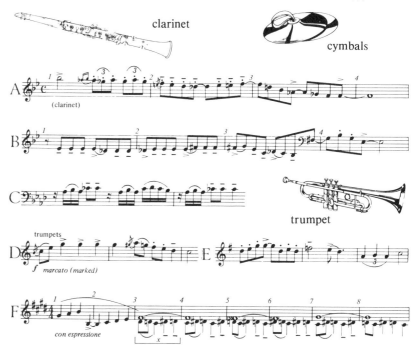

A most interesting record of *Rhapsody in Blue* was issued in 1977, by the Columbia Jazz Band conducted by Michael Tilson Thomas, with the composer himself as soloist. Gershwin died in 1937; Michael Tilson Thomas was born in 1944 – so you may wonder how they managed to meet! It came about in this way:

First, the Columbia Jazz Band recorded Grofé's original band parts. Then the solo piano part was 'dubbed in' from a piano roll which Gershwin made in 1924. Listening to this vivid recording gives one the uncanny feeling that Gershwin was actually there among the musicians at the recording session, playing his music 'live' . . .

Piotr Ilyitch Tchaikovsky RUSSIA 1840-1893

Fantasy~Overture

Romeo and Juliet

Tchaikovsky's father was an inspector of mines. When the boy was 10, the family moved to St. Petersburg – now known as Leningrad. Tchaikovsky – who was extremely sensitive and suffered from acute nervous troubles all through his life – adored his mother, and was deeply affected by her death, from cholera, when he was 14.

It was decided that Tchaikovsky should study law, and also take music lessons at the same time. At 19, he became a clerk in the Ministry of Justice. But four years later he gave up his post to enter the St. Petersburg Conservatoire of Music. He left with full honours in 1866 and became a teacher at the Moscow Conservatoire of Music.

Tchaikovsky's first compositions were not successful. He made friends with the group of composers who called themselves *The Russian Five*: Balakirev, Rimsky-Korsakov, Borodin, Cui, and Mussorgsky. In 1870, Balakirev, who had intended to write a piece based on Shakespeare's tragedy *Romeo and Juliet*, suggested that

Tchaikovsky should take up the idea instead. The powerful, emotional mood of the story immediately appealed to him, but this piece was also a failure – at first.

In 1874, Tchaikovsky began his *First Piano Concerto in B flat minor*, dedicating it to Nicholas Rubinstein who was Director of the Moscow Conservatoire. When Rubinstein tried it over, he made some scathing criticisms and ended up by throwing the music onto the floor, telling Tchaikovsky that it was completely unplayable. Tchaikovsky, bitterly wounded by Rubinstein's comments, tore up the dedication – fortunately not the music itself, which has become the best-loved and most often played Piano Concerto ever written.

In 1877, Tchaikovsky began to receive passionate love-letters from a young woman called Antonina Milyukova. He visited her to persuade her that he could not love her – but when she threatened to kill herself he became terrified, and foolishly consented to marry her. He ignored urgent advice from his friends, protesting that he was 'a man of his word'. The marriage lasted nine months. Unable to bear his wife any longer, Tchaikovsky took desperate measures – he tried to kill himself by standing up to his neck in the ice-cold waters of the River Neva. But though extremely sensitive in mind and character, Tchaikovsky was very strong in body. He survived. He never saw his wife again, and little is known about her until she died, years later, in an asylum.

Then came the turning-point in his career. A wealthy widow named Madame Nadezhda von Meck, whose husband had made a fortune in building Russian railways, offered him a salary of 6000 roubles a year if he would give up teaching to devote all his time to composing. There was one rather strange condition – that he should never try to meet her. Tchaikovsky agreed. But though they never met, many letters passed between them, describing in detail Tchaikovsky's thoughts and feelings about his music. This lasted for thirteen years. Then the payments, and – to Tchaikovsky's sorrow – the letters as well, suddenly ceased. He never heard from Madame von Meck again.

Tchaikovsky was extremely self-critical, but easily depressed when others criticised his music. When the *Pathétique*, his last symphony, was received without much enthusiasm, he visited his brother in a state of deep depression. In his agitation, he seized a glass of unboiled water and drank deeply. During the evening he became very feverish. A doctor was called. A week later, it was announced that Tchaikovsky – like his mother before him – had died of cholera.

The story

> Two households, both alike in dignity,
>   In fair Verona, where we lay our scene,
> From ancient grudge break to new mutiny,
>   Where civil blood makes civil hands unclean.
> From forth the fatal loins of these two foes
>   A pair of star-cross'd lovers take their life;
> Whose misadventured piteous overthrows
>   Doth with their death bury their parents' strife . . .

Shakespeare's 'two households' are the Montagues and Capulets – two noble families living in 16th century Verona, a town in Northern Italy. Because of an ancient quarrel they are bitter enemies and chance meetings inevitably lead to sword-fights and death.

Lord Capulet arranges a masked ball. Romeo, a Montague, and his two friends Mercutio and Benvolio, decide to 'gate-crash'. During the festivities, Romeo dances with Juliet, who is Lord Capulet's daughter. They immediately fall in love. When the guests have departed, Romeo lingers in the dark garden. Juliet appears on the balcony outside her bedroom, and during the love scene which follows, they decide to ask Friar Laurence to marry them in secret – for their families must never learn of their love.

A few days after the marriage has taken place, Romeo is challenged in the street by Juliet's cousin, Tybalt. When he refuses to fight, Mercutio accepts the challenge on his behalf, but is killed. Enraged, Romeo draws his sword and avenges his friend by killing Tybalt. As a result, he is banished from Verona for ever.

Lord Capulet, ignorant of Juliet's marriage with Romeo, arranges that she should marry a young nobleman named Paris. In despair, Juliet appeals to Friar Laurence for help. He gives her a potion which will make her appear dead. Meanwhile, he sends a message to Romeo, telling him to come by night to rescue Juliet from her tomb. But one of Romeo's friends, hearing of Juliet's 'death', rides swiftly on horseback to bring him the news – easily overtaking Friar Laurence's messenger who is travelling by mule.

Romeo, believing Juliet to be truly dead, enters the Capulet's vault in the darkness. He removes the cover of Juliet's tomb to gaze on her face for the last time – then takes poison, and dies. Juliet revives. Realising what has happened, she kills herself with Romeo's dagger.

The love scene on Juliet's balcony, from Zefirelli's film of Shakespeare's *Romeo and Juliet*

(below) Sword-fight in the streets of Verona

violin

cor anglais

'A glooming peace this morning with it brings;
  The sun for sorrow will not show his head.
Go hence, to have more talk of these sad things.
  Some shall be pardon'd and some punished;
For never was a story of more woe
Than this of Juliet and her Romeo.'

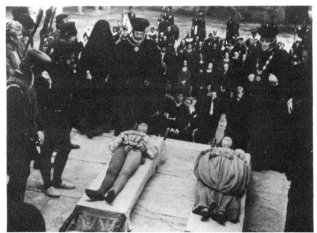

The two families
drawn together by
the deaths of
Romeo and Juliet

In *Romeo and Juliet*, Tchaikovsky does not present the whole of Shakespeare's story, but arranges key events to form a dramatic musical structure. He portrays the strong emotional impact of the story by those special means which have always made him one of the world's best-loved composers – appealing melodies, emotional and dramatic harmonies, and an amazing gift for vivid orchestration.

Points to listen for

1. Slow introduction. Clarinets and bassoons play Friar Laurence's theme (**A**). There are solemn phrases for strings; then a rising tune for intertwined flutes and clarinets above winding cellos, followed by spread harp chords. All this is repeated with changed orchestration.

2. Above an ominous drum-roll, strings hint darkly at future tragedy. The pace quickens. The brass join in, and there is a dramatic crash on the kettledrums. Chords, alternating between strings and woodwind gradually quickening, lead suddenly into the main part of the Overture.

3. The strong, rhythmic first theme (**B**) represents the bitter quarrel between the two families, and the fighting in the streets. A hurrying phrase (**C**) is passed between strings and woodwind. There are strongly syncopated chords – sharply accenting weaker beats.

4. The fight theme (**B**) returns, *fortissimo*, the syncopated effect now emphasised even further by strong cymbal clashes, representing the vicious cut and thrust of the swords.

5. The mood becomes calmer and melts into the love music of the balcony scene (Theme **D**: muted violas and cor anglais). Muted violins suggest the scented darkness of the warm summer night in Juliet's garden (**E**). When Theme **D** returns there is a throbbing counter-melody for solo horn.

6. We hear the sword-fighting music again (**B**) and against this, Friar Laurence's theme (**A**): first on horns; later on two trumpets, battling alone against the opposition of the entire orchestra (Music **F**).

7. When Tune **E** is next heard – on oboes and clarinets – there are short repeated phrases below for violins, restless and uneasy.

8. The love theme (**D**) for full orchestra, but the pulsing woodwind rhythm and horn counter-melody now sound feverish – desperate even.

9. The fighting breaks out once more (**B**) followed by Friar Laurence's theme (**A**), now for full brass.

10. The music rises to its final climax, then sinks into a *coda* based on bars 6 and 7 of the love theme (**D**), beginning with muffled drum beats to mark the tragic end of Romeo and Juliet . . .

Leonard Bernstein AMERICA Born 1918

Music from
WEST SIDE STORY

Leonard Bernstein has been described as one of the most versatile musicians of the twentieth century. He is probably best known as an orchestral conductor; but he is also a brilliant pianist, an author, and has given many talks about music on television. As a composer he has written an amazing amount of music, both 'popular' and 'serious'.

Besides *West Side Story* he has written other musicals, including *On The Town* and *Candide*, and the music for the film *On The Waterfront*. His more serious compositions include three symphonies, two ballets: *Fancy Free* and *Facsimile*, and the exciting and rhythmic *Chichester Psalms*, written for Chichester Cathedral in 1965.

There is a great variety of musical styles among these compositions and some people complain of a lack of depth, saying that Bernstein's music probably will not last. But as an American critic has written: *'There is much to enjoy in his music. It may not be for the ages, but it is superbly for the moment.'*

It was in the early 1950s that the brilliant American dance director, Jerome Robbins, first took the idea of creating a modern 'musical' – a play with music, songs and dances – based upon Shakespeare's tragic drama, *Romeo and Juliet*. To give it even more meaning and impact for a modern audience, he brought the story up to date and set it on the dreary yet violent West Side of New York City. The 'two households both alike in dignity' of Shakespeare's 16th century Verona become two rival teenage street-gangs. Romeo becomes Tony, a member of the Jets, the gang led by Riff; Juliet becomes Maria, a beautiful Puerto Rican immigrant whose brother, Bernardo, is leader of the Sharks. Instead of the glittering masked ball of the Capulets we have a noisy, feverish Dance at the Gym – the shabby gymnasium of a local youth club. And the famous love scene on the balcony overlooking Juliet's garden now takes place on the rusty fire-escape of a squalid block of tenements.

Yet the basic ingredients of the story, which has captured and moved audiences for centuries, remains the same – a tender story of the secret love of two young people, and their innocent, futile hopes for a better future. A story set in the midst of bitterness, violence and danger, which must inevitably end in tragedy . . .

17

1. Prologue (5.00 p.m. The street)

The Jets fear the growing influence of the Sharks in what they consider to be 'their' territory. The rival gangs meet in the street (Music **A** – the first three notes are an important musical idea, representing the conflict between the two gangs. This idea is heard often throughout the whole work – in fact, Bernstein sometimes builds whole pieces out of it). The gangs provoke each other with arrogant finger-snaps, jeers, whistles. A Shark trips a Jet. In a flash, the taunting changes to open aggression, eventually broken up by the sound of a police whistle.

Riff, leader of the Jets, determines to challenge his opposite number, Bernardo, that night at the Dance. He goes to ask his friend Tony to help. Tony agrees – but with reluctance. He has rather grown away from the gang, sensing that life has more to offer than roaming the streets and getting into fights with the Sharks.

2. Something's Coming

Could be! Who knows?	Who knows?
There's something due any day;	It's only just out of reach,
I will know right away,	Down a block, on a beach,
Soon as it shows.	Under a tree . . .
It may come cannon-balling	I got a feeling
Down through the sky,	There's a miracle due,
Gleam in its eye,	Gonna come true,
Bright as a rose!	Coming to me!

3. The Dance at the Gym (10.00 p.m.)

The mood as Jets and Sharks arrive is tense, nervous, ready for action. The first dance is a *Blues* in hard rock rhythm. This is followed by a hot, rhythmic *Mambo* with violent dance-gestures and coarse shouts. Then the frantic rhythms dissolve into a cool *Cha-Cha*. Tony and Maria slowly approach each other as if in a dream. They sway, gently, without touching, to the hypnotic rhythm of the dance – totally unaware of time or place, aware only of each other.

But Bernardo has noticed that his sister, Maria, is dancing with one of the Jets, and strides in icy rage towards Tony. Another dance begins called a *Jump*, with a fast, light, bouncing rhythm. Maria is snatched away, and at Bernardo's insistence leaves to go home. Tony remains absolutely still, lost in his thoughts – realising that he has fallen in love with the sister of the rival gang-leader.

4. Maria

The most beautiful sound I ever heard: Maria . . .
All the beautiful sounds of the world in a single word: Maria . . .

Maria! I've just kissed a girl named Maria,
And suddenly I've found how wonderful a sound can be!

Maria!
Say it loud and there's music playing –
Say it soft and it's almost like praying –
Maria . . .
I'll never stop saying
Maria!

Tony goes in search of Maria. They meet on the fire-escape outside her apartment, and sing of their love in a duet:

5. Tonight (Duet)

Maria: Only you, you're the only thing I'll see forever.
      In my eyes, in my words, and in everything I do,
      Nothing else but you – ever!
Tony: And there's nothing for me but Maria,
      Every sight that I see is Maria . . .
Maria: Tony, Tony . . .
Tony: Always you, every thought I'll ever know,
      Everywhere I go, you'll be.
Maria: All the world is only you and me!
(*And now the buildings – the world – fade away, leaving them suspended in space . . .*)

6. America

The Sharks take their girls home before going to the rendezvous at Doc's drug-store. An argument begins in which the advantages of living in New York are compared with life back home in Puerto Rico:

Puerto Rico, you lovely island,   Puerto Rico, you ugly island,
Island of tropical breezes,   Island of tropic diseases,
Always the pineapples growing,   Always the hurricanes blowing,
Always the coffee blossoms blowing.   Always the population growing . . .

19

7. Cool

While waiting for the Sharks at the drug-store the Jets are becoming nervous. Riff urges them to play it cool:

A dance follows in which the Jets, with rhythmic finger-snaps and easy body movements, 'get cool'. Bernstein writes this in the form of a *fugue*, in which different groups of instruments play the tune, one after another. Tune **H** is the fugue tune; notice that the three-note idea from Tune **A**, marked *x*, plays an important part here, too.

The Sharks arrive. After a discussion it is agreed that the two gangs will meet the following night for a 'rumble' – a fight – on the stretch of deserted ground under the highway. It will be a fist-fight involving the best fighter from each gang.

8. One hand, one heart

Tony visits Maria in the bridal shop where she works. Surrounded by clothes dummies, they act out an imaginary wedding ceremony:

9. Tonight (Quintet)

Bernstein cleverly weaves together the thoughts and plans of Riff and the Jets, Bernardo and the Sharks, Anita, Maria and Tony. All are eagerly awaiting the coming of night – but for very different reasons.

10. The Rumble (9.00 p.m. Under the highway)

The gangs assemble and warily face each other. Tony rushes up. He has promised Maria to stop the fight – but Bernardo turns on him, violently pushing him to the ground. Suddenly flick-knives appear, and the fight becomes a vicious battle. Riff is knifed. Tony snatches his weapon from him and, in turn, knifes Bernardo. The gangs join in, but the struggle is interrupted by the piercing wail of a police siren. The fighters scatter. A distant clock booms as the blinding light from the head-lamps sweeps across the bodies of Riff and Bernardo . . .

11. Somewhere

Bernardo's friend, Chino, tells Maria that Tony has killed her brother. He seizes a gun and rushes out to search for him. When he has left, Tony climbs the fire-escape to Maria's room. She clings to him, in spite of her grief for Bernardo, and together they imagine a place, somewhere, where they will be free from violence and hatred.

There's a place for us, Somewhere a place for us. Peace and quiet and o-pen air Wait for us somewhere.

12. A boy like that

Anita knocks at Maria's door. Tony leaves by the fire-escape and hides in the basement beneath Doc's drug-store. Anita, stunned and broken by Bernardo's death, bitterly criticises Maria for having anything to do with Tony.

A boy like that who'd kill your bro-ther, For-get that boy and find a-noth-er, One of your own kind! Stick to your own kind!

13. I have a love

Maria's answer to Anita is powerfully simple, crushing all argument:

I have a love, and it's all that I have. Right or wrong what else can I do? I love him; I'm his, and ev-'ry-thing he is I am, too.

Tony is given a false message – that Chino has shot Maria. Numbly he wanders through the streets. But Maria is searching for him and at midnight she finds him. Their meeting is brief. Chino appears from the darkness and shoots Tony. He dies in Maria's arms.

14. Finale (Midnight)

While Maria remains kneeling in grief, members of both Sharks and Jets lift Tony's body, and carry him away . . .

Hold my hand and we're half-way there. Hold my hand and I'll take you there Some-how, Some day! (He dies..) (She falters and stops) Some day! dim. molto Maria: Stay back! Te adoro, Anton... (flute) (muted trumpet)

Four Dance Episodes from

RODEO

Aaron Copland's parents were Russian-Jewish immigrants who had settled in Brooklyn, New York. He was their fifth child. The story of his early years is best told in his own words:

'The idea of becoming a composer seems gradually to have dawned upon me some time around 1916, when I was about fifteen years old. Before that I had taken the usual piano lessons, begun at my own insistence some two years previously. My parents were of the opinion that enough money had been invested in the musical training of the four older children with meagre results, and had no intention of squandering further funds on me. But my persistence finally won them over . . . '

In 1921 Copland went to study in France, eventually taking composition lessons from one of the greatest teachers of this century, Nadia Boulanger. He returned to America three years later – with very clear ideas about the kind of music he wanted to compose:

'When I returned to New York after my musical studies in Europe, I definitely set out to write music which everyone could understand was American.'

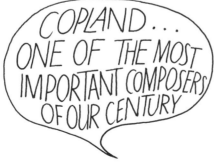

A. Copland

COPLAND . . . ONE OF THE MOST IMPORTANT COMPOSERS OF OUR CENTURY

Leonard Bernstein

Rodeo is thoroughly American, both in its story and in the character and flavour of its music. The story tells of a tomboyish Cowgirl who is in love with the Head Wrangler. But he ignores her, preferring the Rancher's Daughter. The Cowgirl tries to gain his attention by riding a bucking bronco – but he only laughs when she falls off. Then later at the Dance she suddenly becomes very feminine in an attractive dress and with a bow in her hair, and is asked to dance – by both the Head Wrangler and the Champion Roper. She chooses the Champion Roper.

The idea for the ballet was suggested to Copland by the choreographer Agnes de Mille:

'Throughout the American Southwest, the Saturday afternoon rodeo is a tradition. On remote ranches, as well as in towns and trading centres, the 'hands' get together to show off their skill at roping, riding, branding and throwing. The afternoon's exhibition is usually followed by a Saturday night dance at the Ranch House . . .

1. Buckaroo Holiday

'Buckaroo' comes from the Spanish-Mexican word *vaquero*, meaning cowboy. The music is marked *allegro con spirito* – fairly fast, with spirit. And a good deal of the high spirits here are due to Copland's colourful *orchestration* and his exciting use of *syncopation* – putting strong accents on weak beats, where we least expect them.

In this quite lengthy piece, Copland uses several tunes. The two most important ones are:

Tune **A**: a falling scale played by strings and woodwind, immediately followed by powerfully syncopated brass chords.

Tune **B**: a cowboy tune called 'If he'd be a buckaroo by his trade' – first played by a trombone, with *glissandi* (slides) and humorous gaps between phrases. It is then passed around the orchestra. Listen for it to be played as a *canon* (or round): strings, flutes and horns set off, to be chased at one bar's distance by bassoons, trombones and tuba – who are in turn chased by trumpets, oboes and clarinets.

2. Corral Nocturne

A *nocturne* is a 'night-piece' – and the haunting, hushed mood of this music contrasts well with the noise and colour of Buckaroo Holiday.

In five beats to a bar, soft chords on muted strings and muted brass introduce a melody which is heard in a more definite shape immediately afterwards, when a counter-melody is added for oboe and flute (**C**). It is played twice more, with a brief passage for solo oboe and bassoon in between. After each playing of the melody, different instruments add soft chords, almost like an 'Amen'.

oboe clarinet bassoon

flute

trombone

23

3. Saturday Night Waltz

First the string players of the orchestra 'tune up', testing their open strings. Then the waltz begins. It is a slow waltz with a dreamy lilt (Tune **D**) and here Copland uses another cowboy tune called 'Old Paint'. ('Paint' comes from the Spanish word *pinto*, meaning horse.) The tune is first heard on the oboe, helped here and there by the violins – but this is soon reversed: the oboe 'helps' the violins. There are smooth phrases for violas and violins, followed by Tune **D** again – and this time both violins and oboe play the complete melody. Later, there is a long-drawn melody for violas (**E**), with comments high above from clarinet and flute, marked 'lazily'. Then a final playing of Tune **D**.

4. Hoe-Down

An energetic introduction for the full orchestra. Then a catchy rhythm is set going, mainly for piano and wood block (**F**), preparing the way for the main tune (**G**). This is a genuine square-dance tune called 'Bonyparte'. It is given in typical square-dance style to the violins, high-lighted by phrases here and there on the xylophone and clashes on a suspended cymbal hit with a hard stick.

The next tune (**H**), shared between two trumpets, is accompanied by exciting rim-shots on the snare drum, off the beat. (A *rim-shot* is played by placing the left stick with the tip on the drum-skin, the middle of the stick resting on the rim. The left stick is then struck sharply with the right stick, producing an explosive sound like a pistol-shot.)

The dance becomes even more hectic. The noise and the pace are terrific. Then – a sudden stop. The opening rhythm (**F**) starts up again, but the music becomes slower, winding down and down . . . . A short pause – and then a final breathless fling!

Copland has written two other ballets: *Billy the Kid* – alias William Bonney, the notorious outlaw who lived a brief but violent life, dying at the age of twenty-two; and *Appalachian Spring*, which depicts a pioneer settlement in the Appalachian mountains. Both these ballets make use of American folk tunes. Copland's colourful orchestral piece, *El Salón México*, 'evokes the smoky atmosphere of a popular dance hall' and includes several Mexican melodies.

In 1977, an arrangement of Copland's *Fanfare for the Common Man* by the group Emerson, Lake and Palmer reached Number Two in the 'Pop' Charts.

Quiz 1

1. Magic Square

A	O	C	R
N		T	U
S	T		I
L	M	E	B

How many instruments can you find in the Magic Square? Each one must include the letter 'T' at least once – but you can use any letter as often as you like.

2. Who wrote . . . ?
(Name each composer, and his nationality.)
a) Rhapsody in Blue   d) España
b) West Side Story   e) Rodeo
c) Till Eulenspiegel   f) Romeo and Juliet

3. Fill in the Squares

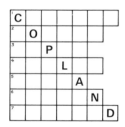

Clues
1. Here the soloist shows off his technique.
2. Special kind of mute for a trumpet.
3. The Champion wins her in the end.
4. Music, dancing, mime – but no words.
5. Heroine of *West Side Story*.
6. Nationality of the composer of *Till Eulenspiegel*.
7. First name of the composer of *America*.

4. X = Y
Most of the characters in West Side Story are counterparts of those in Shakespeare's *Romeo and Juliet*. Can you fill the blanks?
a) Romeo = ...   e) . . . . . = Doc
b) Juliet = ...   f) Mercutio = ...
c) . . . . = The Jets   g) . . . . = Bernardo
d) . . . . = The Sharks

5. Musical Chain
(The last letter of each answer becomes the first letter of the next.)

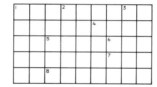

1. His confusion created Kijé.
2. Name given to a piece of music in which the main tune keeps coming round.
3. The English meaning of Till's surname.
4. Italian for 'a joke'.
5. Music + singing + acting = ?
6. His dabbling in magic caused chaos.
7. Title of Chabrier's *Rhapsody*.
8. Italian for 'at a walking pace'.

Now invent your own 'musical chain' – making up a clue for each word.

6. Composers' Calendar
When you have matched the dates to the correct composers, one set will be left. To which famous composer do they belong?
TCHAIKOVSKY CHOPIN HANDEL
BRITTEN
(1810-1849)   (1913-1976)   (1840-1893)
(1756-1791)   (1685-1759)

7. On Target

Many Italian musical words end with the letter 'o'. Can you think of words like this, each beginning with a letter around the target? Here are some clues to help:

Smoothly	Plucked	Getting louder
A joke	Very loud	Moderately fast
Slowly	Sliding	

8. Which instrument?
Fill in the dashes to find six instruments:
a) F–U–E   b) C–R–E–   c) –L–C–E–S–I–L
d) V–O–A   e) T–I–N–L–   f) –Y–O–H–N–
–

9. Mini-Crosswords

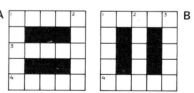

Clues
A 1. (*Across*) Seasonal music – once danced as well as sung.
1. (*Down*) Group of singers.
2. Italian for 'slowly'.
3. Keys, pedals – but no strings.
4. Hoe-down comes from this ballet.

B 1. (*Across*) Tubular . . .
1. (*Down*) A saxophone is made of this.
2. Italian for 'broadly'.
3. Name for a group of pieces.
4. The conductor's copy contains the music for all the instruments.

Giovanni Gabrieli ITALY about 1557-1612

Music from Venice

St. Mark's Cathedral, Venice

cornett

viol

sackbut

Giovanni Gabrieli first studied music under his uncle, Andrea, who was organist of St. Mark's Cathedral in Venice. Giovanni later became second organist and eventually, upon the death of Andrea in 1586, first organist. He wrote a great many pieces, both for voices and for instruments, to be played there.

St. Mark's Cathedral holds a rather special place in the history of music. It had not one, but two organ lofts – set high up to the left and right of the altar. Each loft could also hold singers and instrumentalists, so composers enjoyed writing pieces in which two different groups could be well contrasted. A phrase from the left group would be answered by the same, or a different, phrase from the right – and there were splendidly powerful effects when both groups played together. In fact, the main characteristic of music written for St. Mark's was *contrast*.

Ways of making contrast
By *dynamics* – the contrast of *piano* (soft) with *forte* (loud)
  pitch – high-pitched instruments against lower-sounding ones
  texture – a small group pitted against a larger one
  timbre (or tone-quality) – the gentler tone, for example, of strings and woodwind against the more powerful tone of brass

---

In 1608, a certain Thomas Coryate returned to his native village of Odcombe in Somerset after a journey across Europe of almost 2000 miles – entirely on foot! After dedicating his travel-worn boots to the village church, he sat down to write about his adventures. He was especially impressed by the music he had heard in Venice:

'Sometimes there sung sixteene or twenty men together, having their master to keepe them in order; and when they sung, the musitians played also. Sometimes sixteene played together upon their instruments, tenne Sagbuts, foure Cornetts, and two Viol de Gambas of an extraordinary greatness; sometimes tenne: six Sagbuts and foure Cornetts . . . . That nights musicke continued three whole howers at the least. . . .'

Until the end of the sixteenth century, instruments had been mainly used to accompany voices. But just before 1600 – in Italy in particular – composers began to write pieces for groups of instruments alone. At first they took vocal pieces as their models. An instrumental arrangement of a French song was called a *canzona* (or *canzon*). An instrumental piece in the rather more solemn style of church music might be called a *sonata*. Later on, the word *sonata* came to have a special meaning, but at this time it simply meant a piece to be played on instruments – 'sounded' (*sonata*) rather than 'sung' (*cantata*).

The instruments which the Venetian composers used in their pieces included: viols, violins (which were then relatively new), recorders, lutes, cornetts, sackbuts, harpsichords and organs. The curved *cornett* (quite different from the modern cornet) was made of ivory, sometimes of wood covered with leather. It had finger-holes like a recorder, but a trumpet-like mouthpiece. Played softly, the tone was gentle; but played louder, it could sound as bright as a trumpet. *Sackbut* was a name given by the English to the old kind of trombone. The 'bell' was rather less flared, giving the instrument a softer tone. (Cornetts are often replaced in modern performances of this music by trumpets, and sackbuts by trombones.)

Sonata Pian' e Forte

This is the very first instrumental composition to have markings on the music to indicate contrasts between *piano* (soft) and *forte* (loud). It is also one of the first pieces in which the composer states exactly which instruments are to be used. Gabrieli writes his music for two contrasting groups of instruments. In each group, the three lower instruments are trombones (Coryate's 'Sagbuts'). But in the first group the top part is for cornett; and in the second, the top part is marked *violino* – an instrument more like the modern viola than the violin. Gabrieli obtains contrasts in tone by sometimes alternating the groups, sometimes allowing them to play together. When each group plays alone, the marking is *piano*; when the groups combine, the marking is *forte*. Music **A** shows how the piece begins (*coro*, meaning 'choir', was equally applied to a group of voices or a group of instruments). At bar 14 the second group takes over (**B**). And at bar 26 both play together (**C**).

Listen for the two groups to answer each other in quick alternation (**D**; later **E**). (This passing to and fro of ideas between the groups is called *antiphony*.) Gabrieli ends his *Sonata* with a lengthy section, combining both groups to achieve a splendidly rich, full sound.

Canzon Primi Toni à 8 (Torchi Collection: No. 1)

At the end of the sixteenth century music was still being written in *modes*. A mode is a kind of scale. You can play a mode on the piano by starting on any note, then going up the scale – but using the *white* notes only. *Primi Toni* means 'first mode', which was the one beginning on the note D. *À 8* means 'for 8 instrumental parts', in this case divided into two equal groups. This *Canzona* is in seven sections:

1. Music **F** played by *Coro I*, echoed by *Coro II*. Then both groups combine. (The whole of this lengthy first section is repeated.)
2. A contrast in *rhythm* – beginning with the figure:
3. Beginning slightly slower, with music rather like hunting fanfares.
4. A very short section with exciting dialogue between the top parts of each group. (Music **G** shows the whole of 4, and the beginning of 5.)
5. A contrast in *pace* and *metre*: three faster beats to each bar instead of four steady ones.
6. Chords, *ff*, in the rhythm: followed by fast, tricky rhythms. (Sections 4, 5 and 6 are then played again in the same order.)
7. An impressive fanfare-like ending, *fortissimo*, both groups combined.

Antonio Vivaldi ITALY 1678(?) -1741

Autumn and Winter from
The Four Seasons

Vivaldi's father was a violinist at St. Mark's Cathedral in Venice. Although he saw to it that his son received a sound musical training, he encouraged him to become a priest. Antonio was ordained in 1703, and soon became known as *Il Prete Rosso* ('The Red Priest') because of the fiery colour of his hair. But his church career was extremely brief. While celebrating Mass he would leave the altar, then return a short while later. Some claimed that musical ideas would come into his mind and he would slip into the sacristy to write them down; Vivaldi himself later explained that he sometimes suffered from attacks of asthma. Whatever the reason, from then on he was barred from saying Mass so he decided to leave the Church and give all his time to music.

He became Director of Music at the *Ospedale della Pietà*. This was a girls' orphanage – but with an excellent choir and orchestra. The instrumentalists were many and varied, and it was for these musicians that Vivaldi wrote a great deal of his music. Many of his compositions were *concertos* – pieces for one or more solo instruments accompanied by a string orchestra and harpsichord.

The Concerto

We can trace the idea of the *concerto* back to before 1600. The seeds had been planted in the kind of pieces Giovanni Gabrieli and other composers had been writing for two (or more) groups of instruments (see page 26). This idea of strong opposition and contrast led to the *concerto grosso*. In this, the composer still contrasted two groups of instruments – a small group of soloists called the *concertino*, and a larger group of strings called the *ripieno* (an Italian word meaning 'full'). Sometimes the *concertino* instruments played on their own; sometimes they were heard in combination with the *ripieno* group. There was also what was known as a *continuo* part, played by a harpsichord and a low string instrument. The composer wrote only the bass line for the *continuo*. Above this, the harpsichord player was expected to invent chords – to 'continue' throughout the piece to fill out the harmonies when the *ripieno* group was playing, and to play supporting harmonies when the *concertino* instruments played on their own.

A little later on, the idea of the *solo concerto* became more usual. In this a single solo instrument was pitted against the orchestra. The idea of contrast now became sharper still. One of the most exciting things about a solo concerto is the dramatic contrast of one against many – the single soloist against the full orchestra. Sometimes, a concerto was written with a particular soloist in mind, so that the composer was able to write some quite difficult passages to suit him.

Solo concertos were written in three movements (or separate pieces): Quick : Slow : Quick. In Vivaldi's time (which was also the time of Bach and Handel) the quick movements were written in what is called *ritornello* form. *Ritornello* means 'returning' – and refers to the main theme which was played by the orchestra at the beginning, then kept returning after each *solo* section. These *ritornello* sections for the orchestra were marked in the music by the word *tutti* ('everyone'). So a plan of a movement from a solo concerto can be simply written out as:

Tutti 1   Solo 1   Tutti 2   Solo 2   Tutti 3   Solo 3   (and so on)

Vivaldi wrote more than 400 concertos, including both kinds – the *concerto grosso* and the *solo concerto*.

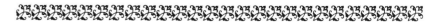

The Four Seasons are four solo concertos for violin, string orchestra, and *continuo*. They are programmatic – or descriptive – pieces. The score of each concerto begins with a poem (possibly by Vivaldi himself) describing that particular season of the year. Vivaldi breaks up each poem into sections. He places a letter of the alphabet at the beginning of each section, and these letters appear in the score at those places where his music vividly describes the points mentioned in the poem.

The first concerto describes the freshness and beauty of Spring. The opening movement includes birdsong and a spring storm; in the slow movement, the goatherd sleeps peacefully, his faithful dog by his side; and the third movement is a lively rustic dance. The second concerto describes the heat of Summer. There is more birdsong – cuckoo, turtle doves and goldfinch – and a quite spectacular summer thunder storm.

Autumn

1. *Allegro* – fairly fast (Music **A** is the *ritornello* tune which returns for each *tutti* section during this first movement)

Tutti 1	**A**	The peasants celebrate with dance and song the pleasures of a rich and fruitful harvest;
Solo 1		(double-stoppings for the soloist, based on Music **A**)
Tutti 2		(a fairly brief appearance of the *ritornello* – Music **A**)
Solo 2	**B**	Full of the wine, the liquor of Bacchus . . .
Tutti 3		(the *ritornello* tune is heard here in the minor key)
Solo 3		(the drunkard continues to stagger and sway . . .)
Tutti 4		(mainly based on rhythm *x* from Music **A**)
Solo 4	**C**	They finish off their merry-making with a sleep.
Tutti 5		(a final appearance of the *ritornello*, to round off the movement in the 'home' key of F major)

2. *Adagio* – slowly

	D	All are encouraged to leave off singing and dancing by the mild air, which now gives pleasure; And by the season itself, which invites everyone to enjoy a soft, sweet sleep.

(There are no solo passages in this movement. The music, in D minor, describes 'the sleeping drunkards'. Strings *con sordino* (muted) play long-held chords, while the harpsichord (*continuo*) player improvises *arpeggios*, or broken chords, across the slow-moving harmonies.)

3. *La Caccia: Allegro* – The Hunt: fairly fast

Tutti 1	**E**	At dawn, the hunters set out with guns and dogs and hunting-horns.
Solo 1		(hunting calls for the soloist, echoed by a solo cello)
Tutti 2		(a brief appearance of the *ritornello* – Tune **E**)
Solo 2		(more hunting-calls, followed by dashing arpeggios)
Tutti 3		(also rather brief – now in the bright key of C major)
Solo 3	**F**	The beast takes flight; the hunters follow its traces.
	G	Already terrified, and weakened by the great noise of guns and dogs – and wounded . . .
Tutti 4		(again in C major)
Solo 4		(the wounded beast weaves desperately from side to side)
Tutti 5		(now in the 'home' key of F major)
Solo 5	**H**	It tries, feebly, to escape – but exhausted, dies . . .
Tutti 6		(a final, triumphant, appearance of the *ritornello*)

Hunt by Night, by Uccello

A winter scene by the Flemish painter, Breughel

Winter

1. *Allegro non molto* – not too fast

(In this first movement there is no real 'tune' for the *ritornello* which returns in the *tutti* sections. Instead, the orchestra builds up discords in F minor, suggesting the bleakness of the wintry landscape.)

Tutti 1   **A**   Trembling with cold amid the silvery snow,

Solo 1   **B**   Beaten by a horrid icy wind,

Tutti 2   (beginning with the discords; then quicker-moving notes):

         C   We run – stamping our feet at every pace.

Solo 2   (brisk running passages for solo violin; broken up later by shuddering orchestral chords, marked *venti* – 'winds')

Tutti 3   (the discords of the *ritornello* return in E flat major)

Solo 3   (arpeggios; then icy double-stoppings:)

         D   Unable to still the chattering of our teeth.

Tutti 4   (recalling the stamping rhythms of Tutti 2 – Music **C**)

2. *Largo* – broadly

         E   To spend quiet and contented days by the fireside
                while, outside, the rain soaks everyone.

(The steadily falling rain is portrayed by *pizzicato* (plucked) semi-quavers on the violins, *pizzicato* quavers on cellos and double basses, and long-held notes played *arco* (with the bow), on violas. Against this background, the solo violin plays a flowing melody, suggesting the warmth and comfort of sitting indoors at the fireside.)

3. *Allegro* – fairly fast

(The last movement, unusually, has no opening *tutti* section. It begins straight away with the first *solo*.)

Solo 1   **F**   We walk on the ice with slow and timid steps,

Tutti 1   **G**   And with great care, for fear of slipping,

         H   One swift move – and you crash to the ground!

Solo 2   **I**   We get up, and again we run on the treacherous ice –

Tutti 2   **L**   Till it cracks and splits with crunchy sound.

Solo 3   (short, violent downward arpeggios for the soloist)

Tutti 3   **M**   Listen! Howling through bolted doors:

Solo 4   **N**   Sirocco, Borea, and all the other Winds, battling . . .

Tutti 4   (brisk, exhilarating solo runs; shivering, shuddering orchestral chords. Above the final bars, Vivaldi writes:)
         This is Winter – but O what joy it brings!

The Italian group, *I Musici,* performing Vivaldi's *The Four Seasons.* The violinist on the left is playing the solo part. Behind him, at the harpsichord, sits the *continuo* player.

A stamp issued to mark the three hundredth anniversary of Vivaldi's birth

(right) The title page of the first printed copy of The Four Seasons. These violin concertos were actually the first four of a set of twelve, called *The Trial of Harmony and Invention*

Wolfgang Amadeus Mozart AUSTRIA 1756-1791

First Movement from

Eine Kleine Nachtmusik

Serenade for String Orchestra

Mozart's title means 'a little night music'; but he also calls his piece *Serenade*, which means 'evening music'. Either way, it is ideally suited to relaxed listening, perhaps after a particularly good meal – for it is likely that Mozart had such an occasion in mind when he wrote it. Serenades were often meant for performance out of doors (sometimes under someone's window) and so were scored mainly for wind instruments. But Mozart scores *Eine Kleine Nachtmusik* for a small orchestra of strings only (like the one on page 31, but without harpsichord). The piece is in four movements, rather like a miniature symphony. The first movement is in Sonata Form, which has three main sections, rounded off by a *Coda*:

EXPOSITION			DEVELOPMENT	RECAPITULATION			CODA
FIRST THEME (in the 'home' key)	BRIDGE PASSAGE (changing key)	SECOND THEME (in a different key)	In various keys but avoiding the 'home' key	FIRST THEME (in the 'home' key)	BRIDGE PASSAGE altered to lead to:-	SECOND THEME (now also in the 'home' key)	or rounding-off

Mozart calls the second movement *Romanze* ('Romance'), and marks the music *Andante* ('at a walking pace'). The tune (**A**, below) flows smoothly and elegantly on the first violins. This movement is written in the design: A B A C A. Section C is a strong contrast – C minor instead of C major.

The third movement is a *Minuet* (Tune **B**) and *Trio* (Tune **C**). After the Trio, the Minuet is played again, this time without repeats.

The last movement is a *Rondo: Allegro* ('fairly quickly') in which the main tune (**D**) keeps 'coming round' with contrasting music between.

The house in Salzburg where Mozart was born

33

Franz Schubert AUSTRIA 1797-1828

Song: The Trout *(Die Forelle)* and Variations from The Trout Quintet

Franz Schubert was the thirteenth child in a family of fourteen. His father, a school teacher in Vienna, taught him to play the violin; an older brother gave him piano lessons. His beautiful singing-voice won him a place in the Imperial choristers school in Vienna, called the *Konvikt*, but Schubert didn't really enjoy life there until he was allowed to play in the school orchestra. Then, his studies progressed rapidly. 'There is nothing I can teach him,' declared the leader of the orchestra. 'He has everything . . .'

Even while at the choir school, Schubert was composing songs and instrumental pieces – but in secret, for he knew his father had strong ideas that he, too, should become a school teacher. When his voice broke, he had to leave the *Konvikt*. He became an assistant teacher at

The original manuscript of *The Trout*. Schubert, working late at night and very tired, picks up the ink-bottle instead of the sand-box (the 18th century equivalent of blotting-paper)

his father's school and for three years taught the lowest class. But his mind was often far away, working on some new composition. 'When I was composing I was always annoyed by those children, who kept disturbing me!' he complained. During his first year of teaching at his father's school, when he was seventeen, Schubert wrote his first really important song, called *Gretchen at the Spinning-Wheel*.

During his brief life, Schubert wrote more than 600 songs (or *Lieder*, as they are called in German). They touch on every possible mood and emotion, and range from simple folk-like melodies such as *Rose Among the Heather* to powerful dramatic ballads such as *The Erlking*. Schubert was one of the first composers to make the piano accompaniment in a song really important. The piano and the voice become equal partners. In *The Erlking*, the pianist plays thundering octaves and chords in groups of three from beginning to end, striking an atmosphere of terror. The voice-part, too, is fiendishly difficult. The singer must change his voice to present three characters – the terrified child, the father who is trying to comfort him, and the dreaded Erlking who haunts the forest through which they are desperately riding.

A drawing of Schubert at the age of sixteen

The Trout

Schubert wrote his song called *The Trout* in 1818, when he was twenty-one. The melody is in his folk-song style, but the accompaniment is not easy to play. The piano must ripple and glitter lightly beneath the voice, suggesting the trout darting and flashing in the stream. Of the three verses, the music for the first two is the same.

For the third verse, the music moves into the minor key as the cunning fisherman muddies the water – and for a while the darting figure in the accompaniment disappears. The trout, deceived, takes the bait and is caught! Then the music returns to the major key, and the accompaniment sparkles once more to end the song.

The beautiful Upper Austrian countryside where Schubert wrote *The Trout Quintet*

In 1820, Schubert went on a walking tour of Upper Austria with his friend Johann Vogl, a singer who had performed a great many of his songs. At the town of Steyr they were guests of an amateur cellist called Sylvester Paumgartner, who knew and loved Schubert's song *The Trout* and begged him to write an instrumental piece based on it. Paumgartner frequently held musical evenings at which his friends who could sing or play intruments took part. It seems likely that Schubert wrote for those particular instruments which were available at the time – a quintet consisting of piano, violin, viola, cello and double bass. Usually, a *piano quintet* is made up of a piano and a string quartet – which has two violins, a viola and a cello. But in *The Trout Quintet*, the double bass (instead of a second violin) adds great depth and richness to the texture.

There are five movements in *The Trout Quintet*. The song itself appears in the fourth movement, where Schubert writes variations upon the melody. The whole Quintet is in a carefree, summer mood with a freshness and beauty inspired by the Austrian countryside where Schubert enjoyed his holiday.

Variations from The Trout Quintet

Theme: The strings alone play the song-melody on which the variations will be based – but there are some changes (Music **A**). The rhythms are slightly different from those of the song, and the key is D major instead of D flat major. The melody is in *binary* (two-part) design: ‖ : A (8 bars) : ‖ B (12 bars) ‖

Variation 1: The piano enters with the tune in high octaves. The music bubbles along joyfully above rich *pizzicato* notes on the double bass; the other string instruments have darting *triplets* – semiquavers in groups of three. In the second part of this variation there are high trills for the violin.

Variation 2: Smoothly flowing triplets are heard on the violin while the tune is played by the viola. The piano softly echoes each phrase one bar later (Music **B**).

Variation 3: Double bass and cello take the melody. The piano flashes and sparkles high above with swift demi-semiquavers in groups of four.

Variation 4: This begins *fortissimo* in the key of D minor, but after four bars there is a sudden bright change of key to F major. In the second part, a figure on the piano beginning with a trill is imitated by the violin.

Variation 5: The cello plays a leisurely version of the melody in a mixture of B flat major and B flat minor (Music **C**). The second part begins in the minor key, then gradually works its way to D major for the last variation – which acts as a *Coda*, or ending, to the movement.

Coda: The rhythm becomes more joyful as – against the melody, shared between violin and cello – the rippling, darting figure from the original song accompaniment appears on the piano. Because of this, the Coda is more like the original song than any of the variations.

Schubert in his twenties

double bass

cello

violin

viola

Ottorino Respighi ITALY 1879-1936

The Pines of Rome

We usually think of music by Italian composers as being concerned mainly with the human voice – especially opera. But the main compositions of Ottorino Respighi are for orchestra only. He was expert in *orchestration* – writing for full orchestra – having taken lessons from the famous Russian composer, Rimsky-Korsakov. Respighi usually asks for an extremely large orchestra, drawing particularly on the brass and percussion sections to provide vivid and colourful sounds. Most of his pieces are *programme music* – which means they are descriptive in some way.

Though born in Bologna, Respighi later went to live in Rome. Three of his best known pieces were inspired by this great Italian city, so rich in history, colour and atmosphere:- *The Fountains of Rome, The Pines of Rome*, and *Roman Festivals*.

The Pines of Rome is made up of four contrasting pieces, played without a break. The orchestra needed to play it is huge, including: 3 flutes and piccolo, 2 oboes and cor anglais, 2 clarinets and bass clarinet, 2 bassoons and double bassoon; 4 horns, 3 trumpets – and one trumpet played off-stage, 3 trombones, bass tuba, 6 *buccine* (the war trumpet of ancient Rome, but imitated here by 6 flügelhorns); kettledrums, bass drum, cymbals, 2 small cymbals, tambourine, rattle, triangle, tamtam (a huge gong), harp, tubular bells, celesta, piano, organ; and a very large section of strings.

There is one very strange addition to this large orchestra. In the third piece, Respighi wanted the effect of a nightingale's song. This is introduced by a clarinet solo, and is accompanied *pianissimo* (very softly) by trills on muted violins, harp notes, and a chord held by violas and cellos. It is at this point that the extra 'instrument' is introduced. It is in fact a gramophone! It is listed in the score, with all the other instruments, as: 'Gramophone – Record No. R.6105 of the Concert Record Gramophone: *The Song of the Nightingale*'. This caused quite a stir when the music was first performed.

The Appian Way in Rome, with its umbrella pines

When asked about his use of the nightingale's song, to be played on a gramophone record during performance of *The Pines of Rome*, Respighi replied:

'I do not believe in sensational effects for their own sake . . . True, there is a gramophone record of a real nightingale's song used in the third movement. It is a nocturne, and the dreamy, subdued air of the woodland at the evening hour is mirrored in the scoring for the orchestra. Suddenly there is silence, and the voice of the real bird rises, with its liquid notes.

Now that device has created no end of discussion in Rome, in London – wherever the work has been played . . . I simply realised that no combination of wind instruments could quite counterfeit the real bird's song. Not even a *coloratura* soprano could have produce an effect other than artificial. So I used the gramophone. The directions in the score have been followed wherever it has been played.'

Page of the score showing the recording of the nightingale

This is how Respighi himself describes *The Pines of Rome:*

1. The Pines of the Villa Borghese

(*Allegretto* – fairly fast, but not as fast as *allegro*)
Children are at play in the pine grove of the Villa Borghese. They dance round in circles (Tune **A**). They play at soldiers, marching and fighting (Tune **B**). They twitter and shriek like swallows at evening. They disappear. Suddenly, the scene changes to:

2. The Pines near a Catacomb

(*Lento* – slowly; beginning quietly with muted strings and horns)
We see the shadows of the pines which overhang the entrance of a catacomb (Tune **C** on a trumpet, off-stage). From the depths rises a chant which re-echoes solemnly, like a hymn (Tune **D**), and is then mysteriously silenced.

3. The Pines of the Janiculum

(*Lento* – slowly; with solos for piano and clarinet)
There is a thrill in the air as the full moon reveals the profile of the pines of Gianicolo's Hill (Tunes **E** and **F**). A nightingale sings . . .

4. The Pines of the Appian Way

(*Tempo di marcia* – at the pace and rhythm of a march)
Misty dawn on the Appian Way. The tragic countryside is guarded by solitary pines. The muffled, ceaseless rhythm of unending footsteps (Tune **G**). To the imagination there appears a vision of past glories: trumpets sound, and the army of the Consul advances in the brilliance of the newly risen sun towards the Sacred Way, mounting in triumph to the Capitol.

THE NIGHTINGALE.

I use nature as a point of departure in order to recall memories and visions...

Respighi

French horn

clarinet

oboe

bass clarinet

trumpet

Respighi's 'companion' work, *The Fountains of Rome*, is also made up of four linked pieces. They describe, in equally vivid sounds, four of Rome's famous fountains, each at a different time of day: the Fountain of the Valle Giulia at Dawn; the Triton Fountain in the Morning; the Trevi Fountain at Midday; the Fountain of the Villa Medici at Sunset.

In his third group of Roman pieces, *Roman Festivals*, Respighi said he tried 'to conjure up visions and evocations of Roman fêtes by means of a maximum of orchestral sounds and colours'. The titles are: Games in the Circus Maximus; The Jubilee; The October Harvest Festival; and The Epiphany.

Respighi's *Suite: The Birds* is a strong contrast in that, on this occasion, he uses a small orchestra. After a Prelude (which has been used as a signature tune for the television programme *Going For a Song*) there follow four pieces: The Dove, The Hen, The Nightingale, and The Cuckoo – each based upon a harpsichord or lute piece by a 17th or 18th century composer.

In 1918, the Russian ballet impresario Diaghilev asked Respighi to provide music for a ballet entitled *La Boutique Fantasque* ('The Fantastic Toyshop'). For this, Respighi orchestrated tunes from songs and piano pieces by his fellow countryman, Rossini.

Sir William Walton ENGLAND Born 1902

Belshazzar's Feast

William Walton

Since the 18th century, British audiences have shown a fondness for oratorios. Handel found his oratorios to be every bit as popular as his operas, even though they lacked the spectacle of costumes and scenery. In the 19th century, the oratorios of Mendelssohn made an impact in England – especially *Elijah*, with its flowing arias such as 'O rest in the Lord' and the dramatic chorus: 'O Baal, we cry to thee!'.

This sparked off hundreds of oratorios by British composers at the end of the 19th and the beginning of the 20th centuries. Some, like Elgar's *The Dream of Gerontius*, contained beautiful and exciting music, but many were dull – performed once, then forgotten. The famous playwright George Bernard Shaw, who had also been a music critic, dismissed them as 'each one drearier than the one before'.

So when it was announced that a new oratorio, *Belshazzar's Feast* by William Walton, was to be performed at Leeds in 1931, few people showed particular interest. Those who remembered his witty and clever *Façade* and the beautiful, melancholy *Viola Concerto*, were intrigued to hear how he would tackle a story from the Bible. But many others expected 'just another British oratorio'. They were all taken by surprise.

Facade had been Walton's first triumph in 1922. He called the work an 'entertainment' with music written to poems by Edith Sitwell. In 1929, Walton asked her brother, Osbert Sitwell, to select passages from the Old Testament for an oratorio. For the main part of his text, Sitwell made an adaptation of the fifth chapter of the Book of Daniel, telling the story of Belshazzar the King and the fall of his mighty city of Babylon. But Sitwell also chose passages from Isaiah, Psalm 137 (the lament of the captive Hebrews by the waters of Babylon), and Psalm 81 (the Hebrews' hymn of triumph over the fallen city).

Walton responded with music that is colourful and imaginative, like the bold strokes of a vivid oil painting – yet music which is as direct and simple as the language and expression of the Old Testament itself. There are sharp contrasts: jagged rhythms and harsh discords with crunching brass and explosive percussion, set against smoothly flowing sections with wistful harmonies, sometimes for voices alone while the huge orchestral forces remain silent. These contrasts may seem more suited to a theatre than a church – in fact, in 1932, *Belshazzar's Feast* was suggested for performance at the Three Choirs' Festival, but was turned down as being 'unsuitable for performance in a cathedral'.

What is an oratorio?

You have probably heard pieces from Handel's *Messiah* – very likely 'The Hallelujah Chorus', or perhaps 'The Trumpet shall sound'. *Messiah* is an *oratorio* – a setting of religious words for solo singers, chorus and orchestra. But unlike an opera, there are no costumes or scenery. An oratorio is not acted – it is just sung.

There are *choruses*; and – for the soloists – *arias* (Italian for 'airs', or songs), and passages called *recitative*. In a recitative there is not much 'tune'. Instead, the melodic line closely follows the rise and fall of speech and the natural rhythm of the words. The purpose of recitative is to 'tell the story'. Arias are more tuneful and flowing; while choruses can be thoughtful – or vividly describe the more dramatic and exciting events in the story.

Walton's oratorio falls into several sections, separated by brief pauses. The first section begins with Isaiah's prophecy:

'Thus spake Isaiah . . . Howl ye, therefore, for the day of the Lord is at hand!

(trombone fanfare, followed by the male voices of the choir in discordant harmonies). It continues with the lament of the Hebrews, captives to the mighty city of Babylon – the female voices now joining in with more poignant flowing harmonies:

Later, the music builds to a climax as the Hebrews fervently proclaim their belief in the eventual destruction of Babylon:

> O daughter of Babylon who art to be destroyed.
> Happy shall he be that taketh thy children
> And dasheth them against a stone,
> For with violence shall that great city of Babylon
>> Be thrown down
> And shall be no more at all.

Then follows the main section of the piece – Sitwell's dramatisation of the Old Testament story of Belshazzar's barbaric feast. The baritone sings an unaccompanied recitative, telling of the riches of Babylon:

Belshazzar's Feast by Rembrandt

All manner vessels of ivory,
All manner vessels of most precious wood,
Of brass, iron, and marble,
Cinnamon, odours and ointments,
Of frankincense, wine and oil,
Fine flour, wheat, and beasts,
Sheep, horses, chariots, slaves,
. . . And the souls of men.

The choir, accompanied by the orchestra, vividly describes Belshazzar's magnificent feast (the four-note pattern marked *x* will be heard often during the music):

Made a feast to a thousand of his lords,
And drank wine before the thousand.

Belshazzar, whiles he tasted the wine,
Commanded us to bring the gold and silver vessels:
Yea! the golden vessels which his father Nebuchadnezzar
Had taken out of the temple that was in Jerusalem.
He commanded us to bring the golden vessels
Of the temple of the house of God,
That the King, his princes, his wives,
And his concubines might drink therein.
Then the King commanded us:
Bring ye the cornet, flute, sackbut, psaltery,
And all kinds of music: they drank wine again.

(Choir, unaccompanied, in discordant harmonies:)
Yea! drank from the silver vessels.
(*Fortissimo* chords, mainly for brass)
And then spake the King:

A short orchestral passage – based on fragment *x* from Music **C** – and followed by a three-trumpet fanfare before the King speaks:

Baritone: Praise ye, praise ye the God of Gold.
Choir: Praise ye, praise ye the God of Gold.

Orchestra: *tempo di marcia* – in march time. The texture is mainly of golden, blazing brass tone, with powerful percussion accompaniment.

Women's voices: Praise ye the God of Silver.
   (Listen here for triangle, glockenspiel, piccolo and solo violin)

Men's voices: Praise ye the God of Iron.
   (Listen here for trumpets, brass bands – and anvil)

Women's voices: Praise ye the God of Wood.
   (Listen for xylophone, wood block, and strings *col legno* – with the wood of the bow instead of the hair)

Men's voices: Praise ye the God of Stone.
   (listen for the whip – and short, *staccato* rhythms)

Mixed voices: Praise ye the God of Brass.
   (Listen for trumpets and trombones – and both brass bands)

The music gradually builds to a climax above an *ostinato* – an 'obstinately' repeated pattern – for cellos, double basses, and piano.

Full choir: Praise ye (*repeated over and over again*)
                Praise ye the Gods!

The third section begins in a similar way to the second (Music **C**, and especially fragment *x*). The voices of the choir are raised in jubilant praise of Belshazzar as he is pledged in wine drunk from the sacred gold and silver vessels, ending with the words:
   Thou, O King, art King of kings;
   O King, live for ever . . .

These passages, so vividly and richly scored for huge brass and percussion forces, must have stunned those in the audience at the first performance who were smugly expecting 'just another English oratorio'! *No* oratorio had ever sounded quite like this before!

In the next section, the baritone, unaccompanied, tells of how the fingers of a ghostly hand came to write words of death upon the wall . . .

A slow, eerie accompaniment emerges – single strokes on cymbal, bass drum, kettledrum, and gong alternately, with rattlings from castanets:

The final section of the piece is the Hebrews' joyous hymn of praise upon the destruction of the city of Babylon. First, there are light dancing rhythms in the orchestra with an important part for tambourine.

Full choir:
> Then sing aloud to God our strength:
> Make a joyful noise unto the God of Jacob.
> Take a psalm, bring hither the timbrel,
> Blow up the trumpet in the new moon,
> Blow up the trumpet in Zion.
> For Babylon is fallen, fallen. Alleluia!
> Then sing aloud to God our strength:
> Make a joyful noise unto the God of Jacob.

A small choir – about one third of the full choir – tells of the weeping and wailing of kings and merchants at the fall of Babylon:

Small choir:
> While the Kings of the Earth lament
> And the merchants of the Earth
> Weep, wail and rend their raiment,
> They cry, Alas, Alas, that great city,
> In one hour is her judgement come.

Full choir:
> In one hour is her judgement come.

'And the King saw the part of the hand that wrote . . .'

The full choir is now divided into two equal groups – Chorus 1 and Chorus 2 – and sings, unaccompanied:

> The trumpeters and pipers are silent,
> And the harpers have ceased to harp,
> And the light of a candle shall shine no more.

Then Walton brings his oratorio to a joyous, blazing conclusion, with 'Alleluias' echoing and re-echoing – soaring high above the vivid and powerful sounds of orchestra, brass bands, and organ:

> Then sing aloud to God our strength:
> Make a joyful noise unto the God of Jacob,
> For Babylon the great is fallen. Alleluia!

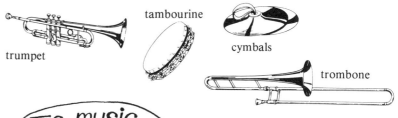

trumpet

tambourine

cymbals

trombone

Sir Compton Mackenzie

The score is a riot of sound, continually pouring in intensity up to the climax where, against a background of percussion noises, the writing on the wall is slowly spelled out. To the ordinary orchestra are added two squads of trumpeters.

Belshazzar's Feast is stark Judaism from first to last, and a jubilant chorus of revenge accomplished makes a powerful finale . . .

The Times, October 11th, 1931

Quiz 2

1. Dial a Composer

'Beethoven speaking'! How many other composers can you find on the dial? Use each letter as often as you like.

2. Tubular Bells

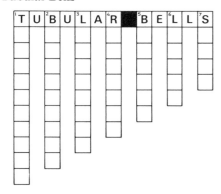

1. His christian names were Piotr Ilyitch.
2. For whom the hand wrote on the wall.
3. The present name for St. Petersburg.
4. Chabrier and Gershwin each wrote one.
5. Plays the broom's tune in *The Sorcerer's Apprentice*.
6. The opposite of *staccato*.
7. Music is usually written on this.

3. Who Am I?

a) POL1810   d) ITA1557   g) USA1900
b) AUS1756   e) FRA1865   h) ITA1678
c) RUS1840   f) GER1864

No, not composers' telephone numbers, nor their car registration numbers! – but their birth-dates, preceded by the first letters of each composer's country.

4. This man is my father's son . . . Who am I?

a) My father was a violinist at St Mark's Cathedral in Venice.
b) My father was an inspector of mines.
c) My father was a village school-master.
d) My father was first horn-player in the Court Opera Orchestra.
e) My father was a composer.

5. Which section?

To which section of the orchestra does each of these instruments belong?
a) Viola   b) Bassoon   c) Maracas
d) Tuba   e) Piccolo   f) Glockenspiel

6. Criss-Cross Quiz

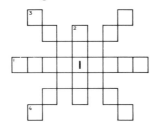

1. Way of playing double bass – without bow.
2. Note quickly alternating with note above.
3. This larger groups backs the *concertino* in an early 18th century concert.
4. A play – with music, songs and dances.

7. Mixed Salad

A. Rearrange the letters to find 6 composers:
a) NOTLAW b) WISHRENG c) TREEBINNS
d) SHEIGRIP e) STURBECH f) FOREVOKIP

B. These are instruments:
a) LOVIN' I   d) RACE LINT
b) MUD RIDES   e) PAXO SHONE
c) BORN TO ME   f) DUN MARRES

C. And these are titles of pieces:
a) DORSET IS WESTY (3 words)
b) THE SPORREN TREE'S CAPRICE (3 words)
c) POEM OF THE SIREN (4 words)
d) EAST OF SUN SHORE (3 words)
e) DAWN TRYST AT HAULZIG (3 words)

8. Rendez-vous!

PARIS   NEW YORK   VIENNA
VENICE   MUNICH   BOLOGNA

Which city would you visit to see the birth-place of each of these composers?
a) Schubert   b) Vivaldi   c) Copland
d) Dukas   e) R. Strauss   f) Respighi

9. In Plain English

Can you give the English meaning for each of these Italian musical expressions?

a) Fortissimo   b) Staccato   c) Alla marcia
d) Diminuendo   e) Tutti   f) Con spirito

10. All my own work

Name each composer, and title of his music:
a) I wrote a 'Spanish Rhapsody'.
b) I wrote a set of four descriptive violin concertos.
c) I wrote *two* ballets about cowboys.
d) I wrote an orchestral piece based on an old legend.
e) I wrote a 'jazz-influenced concert piece'.

Music for Harpsichord

The harpsichord dates back to at least 1500. Early harpsichords had only one *manual* (or keyboard) with one string to each note; but later models usually had two manuals, and three or even four sets of strings. The strings are fixed to tuning-pegs, then run across the bridge to hitch pins fastened firmly to the soundboard.

The basic sound of the harpsichord is of strings being *plucked*; whereas in the piano or the clavichord they are *hammered*. What happens, very simply, is this: inside the harpsichord, at the end of each key, is an upright piece of wood called a *jack*. When a key is pressed down, its jack rises (like the other end of a see-saw), and a small pivoted 'tongue' with a *plectrum* of quill or hard leather projecting from it, plucks the string as it passes. When the key is released the jack falls, but this time the plectrum passes the string almost without sound. When the jack is at rest, a piece of felt called the *damper* prevents the string from vibrating.

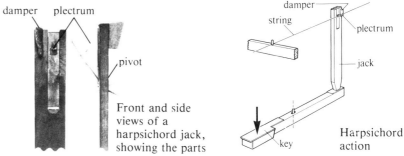

Front and side views of a harpsichord jack, showing the parts

Harpsichord action

On a harpsichord it is impossible to make the sounds grow *gradually* louder, or softer, as you can on a piano. But on a 'double-manual' harpsichord loud and soft sounds, and contrasting tone-colours, are readily available. Other sets of strings can be brought into use by means of hand-stops or pedals. Using these, one set of strings might be played from the upper manual and another set, perhaps sounding an octave higher, from the lower one. Two sets of strings can be coupled together and played from one keyboard, producing a louder, brighter sound. Pulling out certain stops can bring in changes of tone-colour. The warm sound of leather plectrums contrasts with the cooler sound of quill plectrums. A 'lute' stop brings in a special row of jacks to pluck the strings nearer to the tuning-pegs, giving a drier sound rather like a lute. A 'harp' stop causes felt to drop lightly onto the strings, muffling the tone to sound like a harp.

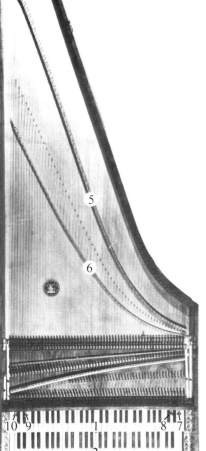

Harpsichord by Jacob Kirckman, London, 1755

Front and side views of a harpsichord jack, showing the parts

On this particular harpsichord there are three complete sets of strings, and four sets of jacks.

1. Upper manual (or keyboard)
2. Lower manual
3. Wrest-plank, to which the tuning-pegs are fixed
4. Jacks – three sets: one for each of the two sets of 8-foot strings (sounding at normal pitch;) one set for the 4-foot strings (sounding an octave higher)
5. Bridge for 8-foot strings
6. Bridge for 4-foot strings
7. Stop to bring in 8-foot strings, playable from lower manual
8. Stop to bring in 8-foot strings, playable from both manuals
9. Stop to bring in 4-foot strings, lower manual only
10. 'Lute' stop, bringing in the fourth, diagonal, row of jacks to pluck the strings nearer to the nuts

This harpsichord has no 'harp' stop. Some harpsichords have pedals to do the same work as the hand-stops – but more conveniently.

François
Couperin

George
Frederick
Handel

Sœur Monique (Sister Monica): rondeau, by Couperin (1668-1733)
Couperin wrote more than 200 pieces for harpsichord, arranging them
in groups which he called *ordres* (rather than the usual name *suite*).
Many of his pieces have fanciful, descriptive titles such as *The
Nightingale in Love, The Little Windmills,* or *The Harvesters* (a
peasant gavotte). Many, like *Sœur Monique,* are designed in the form
of a *rondeau* – an old French word meaning the same as the Italian
rondo. There is a recurring *refrain* (A) separated by contrasting
sections called *couplets* (B, C, and so on), usually bringing in a change
of key. Very simply, the plan of a piece of music in this design looks
like this: A : B : A : C : A : D : A

Sœur Monique is in F major, and the refrain (Music **A**) is always in
this key. The first couplet (Music **B**) is in C major; the second (**C**) in
D minor; and the third (**D**) in F major. The music is marked
'tenderly, not too slowly'. The ornaments not only add decoration but
help to sustain longer notes and give emphasis to more important notes.

'The Harmonious Blacksmith': variations, by Handel (1685-1759).
This is the final piece in Handel's Fifth Keyboard Suite. The title is
not Handel's. Apparently, a young man who was once a blacksmith
opened a music-shop in Bath. He was always singing – and usually it
was this tune of Handel's. Because of his previous trade he became
known as the 'Harmonious Blacksmith' – and eventually the nickname
became transferred from the man to the tune itself.

Handel writes a sequence of five variations on his tune, calling them
doubles – a name given to a simple type of variation which consists
mainly of decorating a straightforward melody. Here, each succeeding
variation is written in notes of shorter value so that the increase in
excitement, as the music gradually becomes more intricate, gives the
impression of increasing speed.

Handel marks his tune: **Air** – and it was no doubt its simple song-like
quality which appealed to the 'Harmonious Blacksmith' of Bath. It is
in *binary* design (two-part: AB), each part repeated (Music **E**).
Double 1: a simpler version of the tune is heard among smoothly
flowing semiquavers (Music **F**).
Double 2: the semiquavers move down to the left hand while the tune
now appears in the middle of the texture, as if sung by an alto voice
(**G**). In the second part of this variation, trills in the right hand are
followed by rather tricky decorations in the left (Music **H**).
Double 3: the tune is hidden away among fast-moving semiquaver
triplets – three semiquavers played in the time of two (Music **I**).
Double 4: the triplets now move down to the bass, and the tune again
appears in the alto line (Music **J**).
Double 5: the tune disappears! But it is still strongly *suggested,* as
Handel keeps the same chord scheme. Rushing demi-semiquavers for
the right hand, then left (Music **K**), bring the variations to a sweeping
finish in an exciting display of keyboard fireworks.

Some players like to vary the sound of the harpsichord, especially
when playing repeat sections, by using a different *registration* –
bringing other strings and other plectrums into use, and so achieving
contrasts in volume and tone-colour. But there are other players who
say that this makes for a rather fussy effect, and who prefer to keep
to the same registration from the beginning of a piece to the end.

A double-manual harpsichord by
John Broadwood, made in 1799

Domenico Scarlatti

Sonata in D minor (L413; Kk9), 'Pastorale', by Scarlatti (1685-1757)
Domenico Scarlatti (born the same year as Bach and Handel) wrote about 550 sonatas for harpsichord, most of them single-movement pieces, very effectively written for the keyboard. They include swift runs, leaps, quickly repeated notes, and sometimes tricky passages for crossed hands. Scarlatti became very annoyed as he grew older (and stouter) to find he could no longer manage to play these!

The *'Pastorale' Sonata* is fresh yet wistful in mood. The title is not the composer's but was given to the music by the pianist Tausig. Like most of Scarlatti's sonatas, it is in a special kind of *binary form*:

‖ : A : ‖ : B : ‖

In Section A there are two themes. The *First Theme*, in the 'home' key of D minor, eventually changes key to F major for the *Second Theme*:

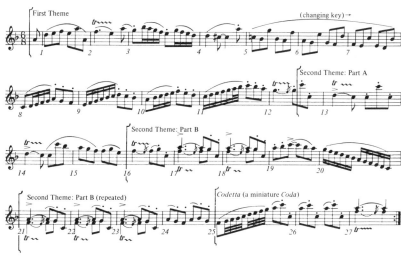

In Section B, Scarlatti develops, or works out, these themes, passing through new keys. Then the *Second Theme* returns in the 'home' key of D minor. The *codetta* now becomes a *coda* to round off the whole piece.

Fryderyk Chopin POLAND 1810-1849

Music for Piano

A portrait of Chopin by the
French painter, Delacroix

Although Chopin's mother was Polish, his father came from the French province of Lorraine. The boy's musical talents were soon recognised. At the age of four he began to receive piano lessons from his sister, and gave his first public concert, playing a difficult piano concerto, on his eighth birthday. At fifteen he had his first piece of music published. A year later, Chopin left school to attend the Warsaw Conservatoire of Music, and there he fell in love with a singer called Constantia Gladkowska. But to gain true recognition as both pianist and composer, Chopin realised that he must travel. When he left Poland for Vienna in 1830, friends presented him with a cup filled with Polish soil. Chopin was never to see Constantia – or Poland – ever again.

A year later, Chopin moved to Paris. Here he met many famous writers, artists and musicians, and made friends with the Hungarian composer, Liszt, and the French painter, Delacroix. His music and his marvellous piano-playing brought him a great deal of attention – but insufficient money. To earn more, he gave piano lessons. In 1835, Chopin travelled to Carlsbad to meet his parents whom he had not seen for five years. On the way back to Paris he met – and fell in love with – Maria Wodzinska, the daughter of a Polish count. Though famous, Chopin was not rich enough to be considered a suitable match. The affair ended unhappily.

Back in Paris, Chopin met the authoress, George Sand. Their opposite personalities were immediately attracted, and this love affair lasted for the next ten years. But in 1838 Chopin became desperately ill with the tuberculosis which was eventually to kill him. With George Sand to nurse and watch over him, Chopin visited Majorca, hoping the climate would improve his condition. When the inhabitants, terrified they might catch the disease, demanded that he should leave, the lovers moved to the deserted monastery of Valldemosa. Although scarcely ideal surroundings for a sick man, it was here that Chopin composed some of his finest music. When they returned to Paris, George Sand's son and daughter schemed to end the affair.

In 1848, Chopin made two visits to England, but loneliness – and the terror of realising that he was slowly dying – drove him back to Paris, where he died on October 17th the following year. Exactly one year later, a monument to him was unveiled, and a small box of Polish earth was sprinkled upon his grave – so that it might be said that he lay beneath Polish soil. . .

Polonaise in A major, Opus 40 No. 1: 'The Military Polonaise'

A *polonaise* is a Polish processional dance, very stately in character, with three beats to a bar; phrases have a habit of ending strongly on the *second* beat of a bar, rather than the first. Chopin left Poland in 1830 never to return – but his country was never far from his thoughts. In his Polonaises, he conjures up a vivid picture of the chivalry and pageantry of Poland's troubled history. The very first piece Chopin is known to have written is a Polonaise in G minor – at the age of seven. The Polonaise in A major is called *The Military Polonaise* because of the strong, war-like rhythm of its first section (Tune **A**). The piece is written in *ternary* (three-part) design: ABA. The accompaniment to Tune **B** is a typical polonaise rhythm:

On the right, you can see Chopin's manuscript. Bar 11 is interesting. In the heat of the moment he continues to write semiquavers – then impatiently crosses them out, correcting them to quavers.

Zelazowa Wola:
Chopin's birth-place

Nocturne No. 5 in F sharp major

The first *nocturnes* for piano were written by the Irishman, John Field. A *nocturne* is a 'night-piece', often expressing the associated ideas of calm, mystery, or moonlight. In Chopin's nocturnes, the left hand part relies on careful use of the sustaining pedal; while above, the right hand sings a flowing melody. The dreamy, romantic style of writing found in the nocturnes – particularly the way he decorates a melody when it is repeated – earned Chopin the title: 'poet of the piano'. The Nocturne in F sharp is in *ternary* form. The first section (Tune **C**) is marked 'sweet and expressive'. A new idea in C sharp minor links to the middle section (Tune **D**), marked 'double the speed' and made up of semiquavers in groups of five. This stormy section suggests that ideas connected with night are not necessarily peaceful. Then the first tune returns, now elaborately decorated like a piece of fine lace (Music **E**).

49

Contemporary caricature
of George Sand

Mazurka No. 5 in B flat major, Opus 7 No. 1

Whereas the *polonaise* was a dance of the Polish nobility, the
mazurka was a peasant round-dance, originally sung as well as
danced. It has three beats to a bar, often with an accent on the third
beat. Chopin wrote more than 60 mazurkas, spread throughout his
brief life, as if he were constantly trying to preserve a link with his
home-land, however frail. His last composition, a Mazurka in F
minor, remained unfinished when he died. Mazurka No. 5 in B flat
major is in simple *rondo* form:

‖ : A : ‖ : B A : ‖ : C A : ‖

Tune **A** is lively, with rhythmic skips and wide leaps, often landing on
unexpected notes (bars 5 and 6). Tune **B** (in F major) is a contrast –
to be played *legato* (smoothly) and *una corda* (with the soft pedal).
Tune **C** (in B flat minor) rides above a 'drone' – G flat and D flat, in
the bass – as if imitating a Polish peasant playing the bagpipes.

Waltz in D flat major, Opus 64 No. 1: 'The Minute Waltz'

The *waltz,* with its whirling three-beats-to-a-bar rhythm, took Europe
by storm in the early years of the 19th century. Johann Strauss had
just published a collection of waltzes when Chopin arrived in Vienna.
Chopin began to write the first of his own elegant waltzes soon after.
The Waltz in D flat has earned two nicknames. One is 'The Dog
Waltz', because Chopin is supposed to have composed it while
watching George Sand's puppy chasing its tail. The other is 'The
Minute Waltz', due to the fact that some pianists claim to play it in
less than a minute. True, the first section (Tune **D**) is swift and light,
but the piece is more attractive if the pianist plays it *musically*, rather
than trying to break speed records – especially when he comes to the
wistful, more flowing, middle section (Tune **E**).

A bundle of love-letters,
labelled 'My Sorrow',
kept by Chopin

Chopin often played
this piano by the
French maker, Erard

Preludes No. 7 in A major, and No. 15 in D flat major: 'The Raindrop'

A *prelude* is an 'opening piece'. Chopin's 24 Preludes are each written in one of the 24 major and minor keys. Although the Preludes are varied in mood and character, it is likely that Chopin meant pianists to take a selection, rather than play the whole group in sequence. Prelude No. 7 is extremely simple – just two musical sentences (Music F). Prelude No. 15 is called 'The Raindrop'. The story goes that Chopin composed this piece during a storm while staying in the deserted monastery in Majorca. The opening is gentle enough (Tune G) – the repeated note A flat representing the steady drops of rain. In the central section, in the minor key, the repeated note is still heard as an accompaniment to the storm – now sounding like a deep, tolling bell.

The old monastery at Valldemosa

Etude in C minor, Opus 10 No. 12: 'The Revolutionary'

Chopin wrote 27 *études*, or 'studies' – each one intended to improve the player's technique in some way. But however difficult a study is to play, however much it may fascinate the player to solve the technical problems, it is the *musical* qualities which must come across to the listener. And those are the same here as in all Chopin's music: superb melodies, unusual harmonies, and a total 'rightness' in the way the music is suited to the piano. 'Every one a poem!', wrote the German composer, Schumann, when he first heard them.

The 'Revolutionary' Etude was written when Chopin, on his journey to Paris, heard the news that Warsaw had been captured by the Russians. The music expresses his feelings every bit as vividly as the desperate jottings he made in his diary at the same time. The left-hand part is fiendishly difficult and throughout the piece the player must carefully grade the dynamics – which keep changing from *forte* (loud) to suddenly *piano* (soft). After a nine-bar introduction, the defiant theme crashes out *con fuoco* ('with fire') above roaring semiquavers (Music H).

51

John Cage AMERICA Born 1912

Sonata 2

from Sonatas and Interludes

In 1938, John Cage was asked to write music for a ballet to be called *Bacchanale.* The story was barbaric, so he considered percussion instruments to be most suitable – but found there just wasn't enough room in the theatre to take the instruments. Instead, he experimented with the idea of obtaining entirely new sounds from a grand piano.

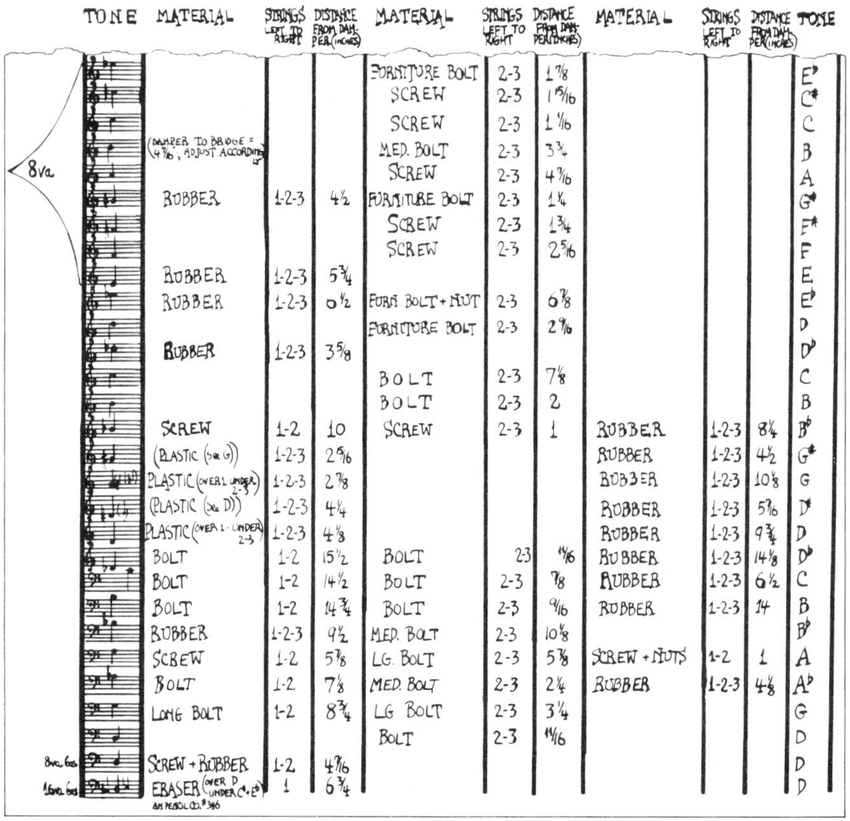

8va

TONE	MATERIAL	STRINGS LEFT TO RIGHT	DISTANCE FROM DAMPER (INCHES)	MATERIAL	STRINGS LEFT TO RIGHT	DISTANCE FROM DAMPER (INCHES)	MATERIAL	STRINGS LEFT TO RIGHT	DISTANCE FROM DAMPER (INCHES)	TONE
				FURNITURE BOLT	2-3	1 7/8				E♭
				SCREW	2-3	1 15/16				C♯
				SCREW	2-3	1 1/16				C
	(DAMPER TO BRIDGE = 4 7/16; ADJUST ACCORDINGLY)			MED. BOLT	2-3	3 3/4				B
				SCREW	2-3	4 7/16				A
	RUBBER	1-2-3	4 1/2	FURNITURE BOLT	2-3	1 1/4				G♯
				SCREW	2-3	1 3/4				F♯
				SCREW	2-3	2 5/16				F
	RUBBER	1-2-3	5 3/4							E
	RUBBER	1-2-3	6 1/2	FURN. BOLT + NUT	2-3	6 7/8				E♭
				FURNITURE BOLT	2-3	2 9/16				D
	RUBBER	1-2-3	3 5/8							D♭
				BOLT	2-3	7 1/8				C
				BOLT	2-3	2				B
	SCREW	1-2	10	SCREW	2-3	1	RUBBER	1-2-3	8 1/4	B♭
	(PLASTIC (see G))	1-2-3	2 5/16				RUBBER	1-2-3	4 1/2	G♯
	PLASTIC (OVER 1 UNDER 2-3)	1-2-3	2 7/8				RUBBER	1-2-3	10 1/8	G
	(PLASTIC (see D))	1-2-3	4 1/4				RUBBER	1-2-3	5 7/16	D♯
	PLASTIC (OVER 1 - UNDER 2-3)	1-2-3	4 1/8				RUBBER	1-2-3	9 3/4	D
	BOLT	1-2	15 1/2	BOLT	2-3	11/16	RUBBER	1-2-3	14 1/8	D♭
	BOLT	1-2	14 1/2	BOLT	2-3	7/8	RUBBER	1-2-3	6 1/2	C
	BOLT	1-2	14 3/4	BOLT	2-3	9/16	RUBBER	1-2-3	14	B
	RUBBER	1-2-3	9 1/2	MED. BOLT	2-3	10 1/8				B♭
	SCREW	1-2	5 7/8	LG. BOLT	2-3	5 3/8	SCREW + NUTS	1-2	1	A
	BOLT	1-2	7 1/8	MED. BOLT	2-3	2 1/4	RUBBER	1-2-3	4 1/8	A♭
	LONG BOLT	1-2	8 3/4	LG BOLT	2-3	3 1/4				G
				BOLT	2-3	11/16				D
	SCREW + RUBBER	1-2	4 7/16							D
	ERASER (OVER D UNDER C♯ + E♭) AM. PENCIL CO. #346	1	6 3/4							D

Part of Cage's chart showing how to prepare the piano

I love silence!
It is as important as sound itself...
John Cage

This is how Cage describes his discoveries:

'I remembered how Henry Cowell had used his hands *inside* the piano – and even slid objects along the strings. So I began to experiment inside the piano myself. I placed magazines, ashtrays, cake tins on the strings. All these appeared to change the sound, just as I had hoped: they made it more percussive – but bounced about far too much! I tried a nail, but it jumped all over the place. Finally, I realised that a large-sized nut or large wooden screw, inserted between the strings, worked best. This completely changed the qualities of the sounds. In a single blow I had discovered a whole range of new sounds – in fact, exactly what I needed. The piano had actually become a complete percussion orchestra, controllable by a single player.'

And so *Bacchanale* was danced to music on a *prepared piano*, as Cage called it. In 1946, he began work on a set of *Sonatas and Interludes for Prepared Piano.* Before performance of these pieces, the piano must be very elaborately 'prepared' – you can see part of Cage's 'Table of Preparations' on the left. Nuts, bolts and screws, and pieces of rubber and plastic are fixed between, under and over certain strings in the piano. The lowest notes of all have only one string each; those in the tenor register have two; and the higher notes have three. Cage carefully specifies exactly which strings are to be treated, and the precise distances from the dampers where the materials are to be fixed. It takes two to three hours to prepare the piano before a performance.

The result of Cage's 'preparation' is two-fold. Not only are the *tone qualities* of the prepared strings affected, according to the various kinds of material used – but also the *pitch*. Wedging material between the strings produces a tightening effect, so raising the pitch. A key normally sounding the note C, for instance, may instead produce a sound several notes higher. Another important effect is that: after preparation, the separate strings of a note may not reach *equal* tension – thus producing two, or even three, sounds of quite different pitch.

Sonata 2

Most of the Sonatas in the set are in *binary form* – like those of Domenico Scarlatti written 200 years previously. Sonata 2 is designed:

‖: A (14 bars) :‖: B (23 bars) :‖

Section A *looks* rather sparse: never more than two notes written to be played at the same time – but many of the prepared notes produce more than a single sound each. The rhythm of bars 7 and 8 is distinctive. Section B becomes 'busier', the right hand eventually bursting into a flourish of continuous semiquavers in groups of three. Again, there are catchy rhythms, particularly at bars 18 and 19.

There is a great variety of sound in this short piece: of *timbres*, or tone-qualities – the preparations affecting the strings so that the piano sounds like an orchestra of bells, gongs and drums; and of *dynamics* – ranging from *pp* to *ff*. The pedals, too, are important. Cage indicates use of the sustaining pedal by a continuous line beneath the music; a dotted line denotes use of the 'soft' pedal, or *una corda*.

Besides his prepared piano pieces, Cage has tried other experiments. For instance, he has been fascinated by the laws of *chance,* and has written pieces (such as his Piano Concerto) which offer performers a choice of which notes to play, and in which order. Such music is called *aleatory music* (from Latin, *alea* – a dice). Sometimes there are no notes at all! One piece, called *4′33″*, is for any instrument, or group of instruments. No one plays a note. The 'music' consists of whatever sounds occur during the 'performance' – which lasts precisely 4 minutes, 33 seconds. *Imaginary Landscape No. 4* is for twelve radios, all tuned to different stations. Each radio has two 'players': one controls the volume, the other adjusts the tuning dial. The effect depends on which programmes are being broadcast. Because of the *chance* element, no two performances of an aleatory piece are alike.

The score of *Sonata 2* in Cage's own manuscript

Karlheinz Stockhausen GERMANY Born 1928

Kontakte *("Contact")*

for electronic sounds, piano and percussion

Like Schubert, Stockhausen had a school teacher for a father. Both his parents died during the Second World War. After the war, he worked as a farm hand, continuing his musical studies at night. Sometimes he earned money playing the piano in dance bands, and on one occasion improvised background music for a magician's act! Later, a music critic named Herbert Eimert had some of Stockhausen's music performed on the radio.

In 1951, Stockhausen married and moved to Paris. There he came into contact with musicians at the Musique Concrète Studios of Paris Radio, where experiments were taking place in 'transforming the whole world of sound sources, via tape, into musical experiences'. Stockhausen was intrigued. But it was not until 1953 – when he was invited to become assistant to Eimert, who was to set up an electronic Music Studio for Cologne Radio – that he became interested in the musical possibilities of electronic sounds.

Electronic music is created by a tone-generator, amplified through loudspeakers, and usually (but not always) recorded onto magnetic tape. Stockhausen's first compositions of this kind were the two *Electronic Studies* (1953-54). Since then, many of his pieces have relied upon electronic sounds – sometimes blended with normal instruments.

Some terms used in Electronic Music

Tone generator: the basic 'machine' which produces electronic sounds

Sine tone: a single *pure* sound (such as accompanies a TV test card)

White noise: a rushing sound made up of all possible frequencies (You can make your own 'white noise' – by saying 'Shhhh. . .')

Filtering: altering a sound by cutting out unwanted frequencies

Reverberation: delay added to sounds so that they die away gradually, blending together – as if in a huge cathedral

Echo: the sound is actually repeated over and over as it dies away

Ring modulator: Combines two or more sounds, and transforms them to produce a completely different sound. Sound and speech can be combined to produce a 'Dr. Who Dalek' effect

---

Kontakte (1959-60) was Stockhausen's first piece to bring together electronic sounds recorded on tape with live instrumental performance. There are two instrumentalists: a percussion player who manages a great variety of instruments whose sounds are made from skin, wood or metal; and a pianist who must also play eight percussion instruments in addition to the piano. The electronic sounds were recorded in the Cologne Studio on 4-channel tape. Stockhausen is very concerned with the *spatial* aspect of music – the points from which the sounds originate. His intention here is that the tape should be played over four loudspeakers set at points completely surrounding the audience. Sounds often zoom swiftly from speaker to speaker, sometimes looping back and forth. The pianist and percussionist, too, are widely spaced apart.

The electronic sounds on the tape were created by tone generator, reverberator, filter, and ring modulator. Although the percussion and piano parts are written fairly normally, the taped sounds are drawn in the score by means of symbols and diagrams. You can see some of these in the extract from the score of *Kontakte* on the opposite page. Sometimes, the electronic sounds are similar to the noise of helicopter blades speeding up and slowing down; sometimes they resemble a car starter-motor trying to function when the battery is flat; occasionally they are as powerful as gigantic space-ships hovering, then passing by.

Stockhausen's aim in *Kontakte* is to seek 'contact' between:

> pitched notes — and noises
> instrumental sounds — and electronic sounds
> live performance — and pre-recorded tape

. . . and, of course, contact between composer and listener by way of the performers. All this is presented with the greatest variety of tone-qualities and textures – both familiar and unfamiliar.

This last point is important when listening to *Kontakte*. For example, the 'scale' of electronic sounds on the tape ranges from the totally unfamiliar to sounds which become uncannily similar to actual instruments – certain drums, cymbals, huge gongs. At some points it is even difficult to distinguish actual piano notes from sounds on the tape. Contact is thus made between the familiar and unfamiliar. . .

Stockhausen himself says of *Kontakte*, *'The order of events does not follow a predetermined course from beginning to end. Any given moment is neither the result of what comes before it, nor an indication of what is to follow. The emphasis is, rather, on the* **now**. . .'

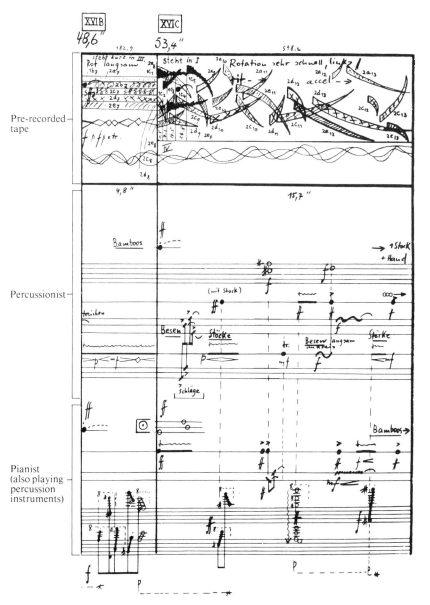

Pre-recorded tape

Percussionist

Pianist (also playing percussion instruments)

From Stockhausen's score of *Kontakte*

Some of the symbols from the score of *Kontakte*

Continuous rotating sounds with no audible attack or decay

Electronic sounds imitating the sounds of certain instruments: bongos, cymbals – even piano

Taped fragments of human voice sounds – vowels and consonants

Long, heavy noise, similar to cymbals, gong or tam-tam

Heavy 'white' noise with greatly varied attack and decay

High or low trill-like sounds

Electronic sounds constantly changing and transforming

Some other pieces by Stockhausen:

Gesang der Jünglinge (Song of the Youths) – the voice of a boy singing the Benedicite is combined with electronic sounds as a setting for the story of the burning fiery furnace from the Book of Daniel.

Zyklus (Cycle) – a single percussionist is surrounded by a variety of instruments. The score consists of several pages, spirally bound. The element of *chance* is present in that the player is free to begin on any page. But he must then follow the remaining pages in strict order, ending with the first stroke of the page on which he began.

Mixtur – the sounds of five orchestral groups are fed through ring modulators. The sounds of the instruments 'live', plus their electronic transformations, result in an incredibly rich *mixture*.

Telemusik – electronic, based on folk music from all over the world.

Refrain – for 3 players (piano/wood blocks; vibraphone/bells; cymbales antiques/celesta). Quiet music is disturbed six times by a *refrain*.

Krzysztof Penderecki POLAND Born 1933

Threnody
To the Victims of Hiroshima
for 52 strings

Krzysztof Penderecki (pronounced Penderetskey) is Poland's foremost living composer. Strangely, music played little part in his childhood, and it was still just a hobby when he began to attend Cracow University at the age of seventeen. Even so, he taught himself the violin and soon began to write pieces to play on it. Later, he decided to make composing his career, and in 1959 entered three pieces, anonymously, in a competition. He won all three top prizes.

Penderecki had literally won fame overnight, and found that his music was instantly in great demand. His success may partly be accounted for by the lack of strict musical teaching in his childhood, leaving his musical ideas fresh and original; but it is also their powerfully dramatic and emotional qualities which attract audiences.

Although Penderecki has occasionally made use of electronic sounds, many of his most striking effects are achieved by asking quite normal instruments to be played in strange and original ways. In *Emanations for Two String Orchestras* – one of the three pieces he entered for the competition – the strings of the second group are tuned a semitone higher than those of the first. The piece is a contest between the two orchestras, and much use is made of *glissandi* (slidings) and other effects where the bow is not used. A year later, Penderecki developed these ideas further in his *Threnody: To the Victims of Hiroshima.*

> On Monday, August 6th, 1945, a new era in human history opened. After years of intensive research and experiment, conducted in their later stages mainly in America, by scientists of many nationalities, Japanese among them, the forces which hold together the constituent particles of the atom had at last been harnessed to man's use: and on that day man used them. . . An atomic bomb was dropped on Hiroshima. As a direct result, some 60,000 Japanese men, women and children were killed, and 100,000 injured; and almost the whole of a great seaport, a city of 250,000 people, was destroyed by blast or by fire. As an indirect result, a few days later, Japan acknowledged defeat, and the Second World War came to an end. . .
>
> (from the Publisher's Note to *Hiroshima,* by JOHN HERSEY)

Penderecki's *Threnody* (or lament) was written in 1960 in memory of those killed or injured as the result of the atomic bomb exploded over Hiroshima fifteen years earlier. In this piece, Penderecki uses sounds for their own sake – and for intense dramatic and emotional impact. He seeks new effects, new ways of drawing new sounds from familiar string instruments, thus sharply contrasting new textures and tone-colours. Yet some of these 'new' sounds are extremely simple – even primitive, as you can see from the table opposite. In some instances, Penderecki crosses the borderline between musical sounds and actual noise.

Sometimes he asks for *microtones* – intervals of pitch less than a semitone; sometimes for *note-clusters* – solid bands of sounds, played by individual instruments, consisting of all the pitches within a given interval – say, from C to G. Massed sounds slide away from each other (*glissandi*), then converge again. All instruments are at times asked to play their highest possible note – lacking precise pitch, but very distinctive in tone-quality. Some of these new effects required new means of notation. Penderecki had to invent his own ways of writing them down, as you can see on the opposite page.

Duration of notes is not shown in the usual way by crotchets, quavers and so on; instead, Penderecki divides the piece into short sections, stating the precise duration in seconds. The page of the score shown here (just over five-and-a-half minutes from the start) takes thirty seconds. The music is scored for 52 strings: 24 violins, 10 violas, 10 cellos and 8 basses. At this point they are divided into three equal but opposing groups. Here, only the first group is playing.

Although most of the music is notated very precisely in the score, there is an *aleatory* (or 'chance-choice') element included. At one point, sequences of symbols are printed with the direction: 'each instrumentalist chooses one of the four given groups and executes it (within a fixed space of time) as rapidly as possible'.

Among these new effects for string instruments, depicting the horrors of the atomic bombing, some notes are actually played in the ordinary way. Set against this tapestry of unfamiliar and often terrifying sounds they have a warmth – verging on anguish – which suggests human compassion for the victims of Hiroshima.

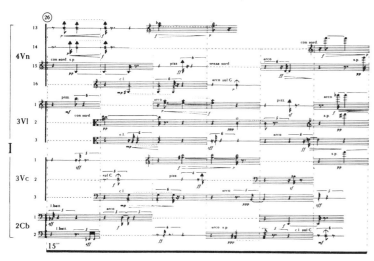

violin   **bow**

Some other pieces by Penderecki:

Three Miniatures for Violin and Piano (1959) – in the second, the pianist depresses the sustaining pedal, but plays no notes. Instead, loud violin notes excite the piano strings to vibrate in sympathy.

Stabat Mater (1961) – words from the 13th century poem (Mary weeping at the Cross) are broken into syllables, shared between three choirs. Whispered effects and anguished cries are mixed with normal singing.

Symphony (1973) – for full orchestra, using every possible variety of dynamics and tone-colours. Note-clusters are used, rather than chords.

Benjamin Britten ENGLAND 1913-1976

The Young Person's Guide to the Orchestra

(Variations and Fugue on a Theme of Purcell)

Part of score showing the percussion variation (Theme E)

In 1946, Benjamin Britten was asked to write music for a film which was to demonstrate the instruments of the orchestra. As he greatly admired the English composer, Henry Purcell (1658-1695), he wrote a set of variations on a tune from the music Purcell had composed for the play: *Abdelazer, or The Moor's Revenge*. Britten called his piece *Variations and Fugue on a Theme of Purcell* – but he gave it a second title by which it is now more usually known: *The Young Person's Guide to the Orchestra.*

The orchestra needed to play Britten's piece consists of:
Woodwind: piccolo, 2 flutes, 2 oboes, 2 clarinets, 2 bassoons.
Brass: 4 French horns, 2 trumpets, 3 trombones, tuba.
Percussion: kettledrums, bass drum, cymbals, tambourine, triangle, side drum, Chinese block, xylophone, castanets, gong, whip.
Strings: first and second violins, violas, cellos, double basses, harp.

The Theme

Purcell's tune is played six times before the variations really begin:
Theme A is for the full orchestra.
Theme B is scored for the woodwind section only.
Theme C is played by the brass.
Theme D is for the strings, including the harp.
Theme E is given to the percussion, with kettledrums playing the first three notes of the tune.
Theme F is for the full orchestra again.

By presenting the Theme in this way, Britten allows us to compare the special sounds of the four orchestral sections, 'framed' by majestic settings of Purcell's tune for the full orchestra.

The Variations

Britten now writes a series of variations based on Purcell's tune for each of the orchestral instruments in turn.

The woodwind

Variation A: flutes and piccolo (very fast). The two flutes set off, accompanied by harp notes, and violins played *tremolo* ('trembling' – with short, quickly repeated movements of the bow). The piccolo joins in at bar 11, accompanied by glittering sounds from the triangle.

The flute

Although it is a woodwind instrument, the flute is often made of metal. There is a hole in the instrument near one end. The player holds the flute horizontally and to the right, and blows across this mouthpiece – rather like blowing across the top of a bottle. This gives the flute its characteristic 'breathy' tone quality. The lower notes are soft and mellow, but higher notes are brilliantly clear. The **piccolo** (Italian for 'tiny') is really a half-sized flute. It plays the highest, most brilliant sounds in the orchestra. Flutes and piccolos have no reeds.

Variation B: oboes (slowly). The oboes play smooth, melancholy phrases above rhythmic string chords. At each climax, marked *largamente* (broadening out) there is a soft roll on the kettledrums.

The oboe

Compared with the flute, the oboe has a thinner, reedy tone. In fact, it has a *double reed*. The player blows between these two reeds, causing them to vibrate against each other – rather like two blades of grass held between the thumbs. The oboe is good for slow, sad melodies, but can sound biting and lively if given rhythmic tunes to play.

The **cor anglais** (or English horn) is really a larger, deeper-sounding kind of oboe.

Variation C: clarinets (at a moderate pace). The bubbling *arpeggios* played by the clarinets suggest a kind of 'musical leap-frog'. In the middle section they show how agile they can be, leaping and swooping from high notes to low and back again.

The clarinet

This woodwind instrument has a *single reed* – a flat piece of cane, fixed to the mouthpiece by a metal band. The lower notes of the clarinet sound rather hollow, but rich and velvety. In the middle register the notes are smooth, while in the higher register they can be quite piercing. The clarinet has an extremely wide range of expression.

The **bass clarinet** – whose shape was later copied by the saxophone – sounds deeper and richer still.

Variation D: bassoons (fairly fast, in march style). Four bars in brisk march rhythm: then the first bassoon plays a *legato* (smooth) melody, to which the second bassoon adds *staccato* (crisp) comments. The rhythm is marked by a side drum, but with the snares lifted away from the skin.

The bassoon

The lowest-sounding of the four main woodwind instruments. The Italian name is *fagotto*, meaning 'bundle' – perhaps because the bassoon looks like a bundle of sticks. As the tube is more than 8 feet long, it is bent back on itself to make it more manageable. The bassoon has a *double reed* – rather like the oboe's, but broader – which fits into the end of a curved metal tube called the *crook*. When played *legato,* the bassoon can sound plaintive; but played *staccato* the notes sound dry, even comic. The **double bassoon**, more than twice as long, and folded four times, plays the lowest notes in the whole orchestra, making a dry, fluttery sound.

The strings

Variation E: violins. A brilliant variation in the style of a *polka*. The violins are treated as two equal groups: first violins, and second violins. Rushing semiquavers and triple-stoppings (chords of three notes to be played at once) are followed by high, sweeping phrases – second violins answered by first violins. The strongly rhythmic accompaniment to the polka is given mainly to the brass. At the end of the variation, the violins play *pizzicato* (plucked) chords.

The violin

The violin has four strings, stretching from the tailpiece across the bridge to the tuning pegs. The strings are normally played with the bow, but are sometimes plucked with the fingers. This is called *pizzicato*. There are several other effects the string player can use, including *double-stopping* – bowing two strings at once; *tremolo* – using short, quickly repeated movements of the bow; and *con sordino* – with a mute. A mute is a small comb clipped onto the bridge to damp the vibrations, muffling the tone.

Variation F: violas. The mood becomes more serious as the darker-toned violas play long rising and falling phrases covering their whole range. There are *staccato* (crisp) chords for woodwind and brass.

The viola

The viola is slightly larger than the violin, and the strings are tuned five notes lower. The viola's music is usually below that of the violin, where the tone is warm and rather dark. It *can* play quite high notes, well up in the violin range, but the tone is less bright, less penetrating.

Variation G: cellos. A variation in very slow waltz rhythm. The long, smooth melody – played off the beat – is perfectly suited to the warm, rich tone of the cellos. (*Lusingando* is Italian for 'pleading'.)

The cello
The cello is roughly twice as big as the violin, but is much deeper from front to back. The strings are longer and thicker, so that the notes are lower, and the tone full and rich. The cello used to be gripped between the knees, but towards the end of the last century a spike was added so that it can rest on the ground. The cello's most characteristic sound is smooth and rich, yet penetrating.

Variation H: double basses (beginning slowly, but gradually getting faster). Though not as smooth in tone as the cellos, the double basses show that they can be quite agile. The accompaniment – flutes, oboes, bassoons, and tambourine – offers a sharp contrast in tone-colour.

The double bass
The double bass has sloping shoulders. It is so large that the player must either stand up, or perch upon a high stool. The strings are very long and thick, so that the notes are very low. When played with the bow, the tone is rather 'buzzier' than that of the cello, but *pizzicato* notes are round and full.

Variation I: harp (majestically). *Tremolo* ('trembling') strings, with soft clashes on cymbals and gong, present a rustling background to full chords, *arpeggios* (spread chords) and *glissandos* (sweeps) on the harp.

The harp
The harp has 47 strings, some of gut and some of metal. But these do not provide enough notes; and so the harp has seven pedals, one for each of the notes of the scale. If the player presses a pedal down a notch, all the strings for those notes are shortened slightly, and the notes sounded are one semitone higher. If the pedal is pressed down to the second notch, the pitch is raised a further semitone. So the player is kept busy with his feet as well as with his hands. Two typical harp 'effects' are *arpeggios* – spreading out the notes of a chord; and the *glissando* – sweeping the finger-tips across the strings.

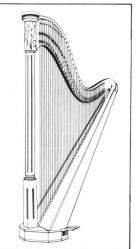

The brass

Variation J: horns (at the same pace). The strings continue to play *tremolo*, and are joined by soft rolls on the kettledrums and ripples from the harp, forming a background to mysterious, echoing horn-calls.

The French horn

The first horn to be used in the orchestra was called the 'natural' horn. It was like a hunting-horn and could only play certain notes. But around 1820, the modern horn with 3 valves came into use. *Valves* add in extra bits of tubing. By using the valves, and altering his lip pressure, a horn player can produce a complete range of notes. Also, by inserting his hand into the wide 'bell' he can flatten any note by one semitone. The tone of the horn is usually round and mellow, but can become quite forceful. If the player pushes his hand well inside the bell and blows very hard, the sound can be very brassy indeed.

Variation K: trumpets (lively). An exciting gallop for the brilliant sounding trumpets – who play short, rhythmic phrases, strictly in turn, to a crisp accompaniment on the snare drum.

The trumpet

The 'natural' trumpet which was in use until the early 19th century, like the 'natural' horn, could only play certain notes. Around 1830, however, the modern trumpet with 3 valves was invented, making available a complete range of notes. All brass instruments can be 'muted'. A *mute* is a cone of metal, wood or cardboard, placed inside the bell. This alters the tone quality. A trumpet mute can make the tone sound much sharper, more metallic.

Variation L: trombones and tuba (fairly quickly, pompously). Striding phrases for the trombones, demonstrating the blazing quality of their tone, are strongly backed by chords for woodwind, trumpets, horns, and double basses. The tuba enters pompously at bar 7, followed by rich, solemn chords for all four of these brass instruments.

The trombone

This instrument is more than 600 years old. The early name for it was *sackbut*. It is the only instrument in the brass section without valves. Instead, it has a *slide* which the player slides in and out to alter the length of the tube. There are seven positions for the slide, each with its own range of notes which the player obtains by means of lip pressure. For special effects, the player can play a *glissando* by sliding the tube in or out and blowing at the same time. There are usually 3 trombones in an orchestra – 2 tenors, and 1 bass.

The tuba

The tuba is the largest instrument in the brass section, and so provides the lowest notes. It has 12 feet of wide tubing, giving the instrument a rich, 'fat' tone. It is rarely given a melody. Instead, it adds richness and depth to the bass line. In its higher register, though, it sounds rather like a French horn. Playing a tuba takes a great deal of breath.

The Percussion

Variation M: Britten writes a longer variation bringing in the sounds of the main percussion instruments. They are heard in this order:

> kettledrums (sometimes called timpani)
> bass drum and cymbals
> tambourine and triangle
> side drum (= snare drum) and Chinese block
> xylophone
> castanets and gong (or tamtam)
> and finally, whip.

The **kettledrums** (or *timpani*) are copper bowls with skin stretched across the top. The skin can be tightened or slackened to alter the pitch of the note. The player can use single strokes, or he can play a *roll* by using both sticks alternately and very quickly.

The big **bass drum** stands on its side. The player can make single 'booming' strokes or play a thunderous *roll*.

Cymbals can be clashed together, or a single suspended cymbal can be hit or rolled with drumsticks, hard or soft.

The **tambourine** is a small single-headed drum with metal jingles fixed around the frame. It can be shaken, lightly tapped, or vigorously hit.

The **triangle** can be struck with the beater to make separate 'tings', or a *roll* can be produced by rattling the beater inside the closed corner.

The **side drum**, or **snare drum**, has two drumheads. The lower one has lengths of catgut or wire stretched across it, called *snares*. When the player hits the upper skin (usually with hard-headed sticks) the snares vibrate against the lower skin, making a dry, rattling sound.

The **Chinese block** is a partly hollowed-out block of hard wood, tapped with a drum-stick.

The **xylophone** has bars of hard wood, each tuned to a certain note. It is played with sticks, or rubber beaters if a softer tone is required.

Castanets are small saucers of hard wood, clicked together.

The **gong** or **tamtam** is a huge metal disc, struck or rolled with a beater.

The **whip** is made of two hinged pieces of wood which are slapped smartly together to make a loud 'crack'.

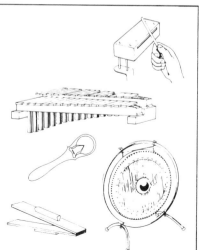

The Fugue

Having 'taken the orchestra to pieces' in the Variations, Britten now puts it back together in a *Fugue*. One instrument begins to play the tune, then a second joins in later with the same tune – rather like a *round*, but a bit more complicated. The piccolo starts off. The flutes join in at bar 8. Then the other instruments follow, in the same order as they were heard in the Variations: oboes, clarinets, bassoons; first violins, second violins, violas, cellos, double basses, harp; horns, trumpets, trombones and tuba; percussion. This is the Fugue tune:

At the end, Purcell's tune returns slowly and majestically on the brass, while strings and woodwind continue to play Britten's lively Fugue.

Quiz 3

1. Instrument jigsaw

Clues Across
 1. Metal bars, hit with hammers.
12. Timpani, or . . . drums.
13. Brass – but with a single reed.
14. The lowest brass instrument.
15. Woodwind – with a double reed.
16. A stringed instrument.
18. You need this to play a violin.
20. A clarinet has a single one.
21. The lowest kind of clarinet.
24. Name given to the width of the tube in a brass instrument.
26. Might be black; might be white.
27. The lowest string instrument.
31. Horns and trumpets have three.
33. Both English and French kinds.
35. A brass instrument.
36. Strings, pedals – but no keys.
37. Keeps the string in tune.
38. Number of slides on a trombone.
39. Strings + keys + hammers = . . . ?
40. You can hit a snare-drum on the skin, or on the . . .

Clues Down
 2. Wooden bars, hit with hammers.
 3. High-sounding wind instrument.
 4. Another name for snare-drum.
 5. Mediterranean instruments.
 6. 'Geometrical' instrument.
 7. Woodwind, but with no reed.
 8. Brass, but with no valves.
 9. Another name for bass drum.
10. A plucked string instrument.
11. Woodwind, with double reed.
17. A clarinet is made of this.
19. Small drum + jingles = . . . ?
21. Tubes, hit with hammers.
22. Might be Chinese.
23. Not single, but double.
25. A kind of horn.
28. Wind instrument with gaudy bag!
29. A trombone has one.
30. Rather like a trumpet.
32. This very special instrument takes it all in!
34. Bass and side are kinds of . . .

2. Order, Please!
a) Arrange these composers in order of birth:
   CHOPIN VIVALDI STOCKHAUSEN GABRIELI MOZART
b) Arrange these Italian terms of pace in order, slow to fast:
   ALLEGRO ANDANTE PRESTO ADAGIO VIVACE
c) Arrange these instruments in order, low to high:
   TRUMPET TUBA VIOLA DOUBLE BASSOON PICCOLO

3. By any other name . . .
Many composers have distinctive christian names. Can you add the correct surname (and country) to each of these? Then mention a piece of music by each composer.
a) Wolfgang Amadeus
b) Sergei
c) Piotr Ilyitch
d) Karlheinz
e) Aaron
f) Krzysztof

4. Just like that . . . !
Which instruments might you play:

a) Pizzicato   d) Glissando
b) Una corda   e) Tremolo
c) Con sordino   f) Col legno

And on which would you play:
g) a 'roll'   h) a 'rim-shot'
i) 'double-stoppings?

5. Who wrote what?
Match each title to its composer, then add his correct country:

The Sorcerer's Apprentice	Tchaikovsky	Poland
Rhapsody in Blue	Mozart	Germany
Eine Kleine Nachtmusik	Chopin	England
Belshazzar's Feast	Gershwin	France
Till Eulenspiegel	Dukas	America
The Revolutionary Study	Strauss	Russia
Romeo and Juliet	Walton	Austria